ROMAN EDUCATION

ROMAN EDUCATION

by

A. S. WILKINS, Litt.D., LL.D.

Professor of Classical Literature
in the Victoria University of Manchester

Cambridge:
at the University Press
1905

CAMBRIDGE UNIVERSITY PRESS
Cambridge, New York, Melbourne, Madrid, Cape Town,
Singapore, São Paulo, Delhi, Tokyo, Mexico City

Cambridge University Press
The Edinburgh Building, Cambridge CB2 8RU, UK

Published in the United States of America by
Cambridge University Press, New York

www.cambridge.org
Information on this title: www.cambridge.org/9781107600515

© Cambridge University Press 1905

First published 1905
First paperback edition 2011

A catalogue record for this publication is available from the British Library

ISBN 978-1-107-60051-5 Paperback

PREFATORY NOTE.

THIS little book is intended in the first place for the use of students. Happily in the case even of those who are preparing to take part in primary education, no inconsiderable proportion have now some knowledge of Latin. I have therefore felt at liberty to quote freely from the original sources, without always adding a translation, although this has been sometimes done. It has not been easy to resist the temptation of trespassing at times on the field of the historian of literature, rhetoric, or philosophy; but I have done my best to keep within the limits imposed by the title-page. I append a list of the best modern authorities. It is only the last of these to which I am conscious of any special obligation, though I have been so long familiar with most of the others that my debt is probably greater than I am quite aware of. With rare exceptions all quotations have been read in and taken from the original authorities.

To the Rev. W. Field and to Professor Summers of Sheffield I owe my best thanks for much kind help in revision.

A. S. W.

MANCHESTER,
    May, 1905.

LIST OF AUTHORITIES.

(1) F. Cramer, *Geschichte der Erziehung und des Unterrichts im Alterthume.* Elberfeld, 2 vols. 1832–8.

(From its suggestiveness and breadth of view not yet antiquated.)

(2) J. H. Krause, *Geschichte der Erziehung, des Unterrichts und der Bildung bei den Griechen, Etruskern und Roemern.* Halle, 1851.

(3) W. A. Becker, *Gallus, oder Roemische Scenen*, Vol. ii., pp. 57–98. Leipzig, 1863.

(Excellent for its compass.)

(4) J. L. Ussing, *Darstellung des Erziehungs- und Unterrichtswesens bei den Griechen und Roemern* (translated from the Danish). Altona, 1870.

(5) G. Bernhardy, *Grundriss der Roemischen Litteratur*, pp. 35–95, 5th ed. Brunswick, 1872.

(Full of interesting points.)

(6) G. H. Hulsebos, *De Educatione et Institutione apud Romanos.* Utrecht, 1875.

(A very good survey of the whole subject.)

(7) L. Grasberger, *Erziehung und Unterricht im klassischen Alterthum.* Wurzburg, 3 vols. 1864–1881.

(A large collection of materials, ill put together and arranged.)

(8) J. Marquardt, *Das Privatleben der Roemer*, pp. 80–126, 2nd ed. Leipzig, 1886.

(An invaluable collection of all important references and quotations, brought together in a narrow space.)

(9) E. Jullien, *Les Professeurs de littérature dans l'ancienne Rome.* Paris, 1886.

Mention should also be made of two recent English works, from which I have not felt at liberty to draw, as covering somewhat the same ground, though the former is much wider in its scope: Professor Laurie's *Pre-Christian Education* (1895), and Dr George Clarke's *Education of Children at Rome* (1896).

CONTENTS.

CHAPTER I.

CHAPTER II.

CHAPTER III.

CHAPTER IV.

CHAPTER V.

CHAPTER VI.

CHAPTER I.

INTRODUCTORY.

THE education given to the children of a nation is of necessity
National shaped by the desire which is commonly felt as to
Ideals. what they shall become as citizens. We can see
this very clearly in the history of education at Rome. In the
free democracies of Greece the aim, at least of those who were
most progressive and most in agreement with the genius of the
nation, was directed to the full and harmonious developement
of the whole nature. That the body should be trained to
strength, activity and grace, that the intelligence should be
quick, accurate, and alert, guided in practical affairs by reason
rather than tradition, that every citizen should bring to the
judgment of the creations of art a trained and sensitive taste,
and should be able to spend his seasons of leisure in music,
song or refined discussion,—to ends such as these the whole
early training was consciously directed. But it
Rome. was very different at Rome. So long as Rome
remained what she was for nearly five centuries of her national
life—a small Italian state, with only rare and limited contact
with the rich and fertile world of Greek culture—the education
of her children aimed at no more than at the developement of
those virtues and capacities, the value of which was recognised
in daily life. If a boy grew up healthy and strong in mind and
body, if he revered the gods, his parents and the laws and
institutions of his country, if he was familiar with the traditional

W.   1 methods of agriculture, and had some knowledge of the way of conducting public business in times of peace and of serving in the field in time of war ; if a girl learnt from her mother to be modest, virtuous and industrious, skilled in the duties of the household, this was all that was needed, that children should grow up what their parents would have them to be. There was no conception of, still less any desire for, any system of progressive culture. The usage of their ancestors (*mos maiorum*) set the standard at which the Romans aimed. What had been good enough for the fathers was good enough for the sons. It was the severest censure to say of a man that he had acted as his fathers would not have done (*contra morem maiorum*). And to maintain this tradition of conduct no system of teaching by outsiders was needed or desired ; the discipline of the home could do all that was required. With the methods adopted the State did not in any way concern itself. Indirectly it did much to hold up a high standard of civic duty and devotion. But the manner in which this should be taught was left to the individual citizen. It has been noted as something of a paradox that while the Greeks were always disposed to look with favour on the interference of the State in questions of training and education, they never secured the same devotion and obedience to the State as were shown at Rome, where the lessons of patriotism were learnt in the home. In the best days of the Republic the training of the children was the concern of the father and the mother, and it was not until the time of the Empire that the State did anything to control or even to assist it.

But as time went on, great changes came about under foreign and especially Greek influence. The better educated classes, in Rome at all events, had set before them a new ideal of culture, and new methods of attaining to it, which fascinated them with their novel charms. All were not equally attracted by them, and for generations there was a ceaseless struggle between the

Results of Greek Influence.

champions of the old and the advocates of the new. But at last the latter won the inevitable and complete victory. Greek methods, Greek models, Greek ideals came to be dominant in Roman education; and these largely in the hands of Greek teachers. Still we must distinguish two periods in the history of Roman education under Greek influence. During the earlier the Romans were gradually learning what treasures of beauty and wisdom were stored in the literature of Greece, and were coming to feel that some knowledge of these, either directly or through the medium of translations, was essential to culture. At a later stage they were no longer content with this; they accepted Greek ideals of culture and adopted Greek methods of training, and these not only for general mental developement, but with direct reference to the demands of public life. A higher stage of education was pursued by all or most of those whose means and leisure would allow it, so that Greek philosophers and Greek rhetoricians came to supply an essential part of the higher education of a young Roman noble.

It will be necessary then that we should follow the histori-
Plan of this Book. cal method, and study Roman education in its successive stages. First will come the purely national stage, when as yet there was no outside influence. Here we encounter at once a serious difficulty. For more than five centuries we have nothing like contemporary evidence; traditions may have been, and in some cases we know that they were, coloured by the usage of later times, and therefore may often be misleading. We must proceed as we do in studying for example the religion of early Rome. If we wish to conceive for ourselves the 'religion of Numa,' so beautifully sketched by Mr Walter Pater in his 'Marius the Epicurean,' we must first take pains to put out of our minds all that we can ascertain to have been of later growth or importation, and especially all that we know to have been borrowed from Greece. So whatever we can ascribe to Greek teachers or methods, we must put aside

when we try to picture to ourselves the training of the early Republic, by which ' rerum facta est pulcherrima Roma.'

Next we shall have to trace the effect in this direction of that great flood of Greek influence, which poured into Rome from the middle of the third century B.C. onwards, and this in the distinct departments of literary—or what we might now call secondary—education, and in the higher training of rhetoric and philosophy.

Then, when we have learnt by what stages and under what influences education at Rome came to be what it was in the days of the later Republic and early Empire, we may study it in the form which it had then taken both in the elementary and in the higher stages.

Finally it will be necessary to glance at the introduction of something like a State-system of organisation and endowment of education.

CHAPTER II.

EDUCATION IN THE EARLY REPUBLIC.

THE younger Pliny tells us in one of his letters (viii. 1, 4-6):
Home Education. 'It was the custom of old that we should learn from our elders, not only through our ears, but through our eyes as well, what we should presently have to do, and by a kind of succession to hand this down to our juniors. Each had his own father for an instructor, or to him who had no father the oldest and most illustrious citizens stood in the place of one.' Pliny is no very good authority for a state of things which had long passed away when he wrote; but he is no doubt right in holding that there was a time when all the education given to children was that furnished by the training—much more physical and moral than intellectual—of the home. But with this training, as we have already had occasion to notice, the State had no direct concern, and did not, as a rule, in any way meddle. Cicero says (*de Rep.* iv. 3, 3), 'with regard to the training of boys of free birth—and this was the only point on which our guest Polybius censures our institutions for carelessness—to which the Greeks devoted much pains to no effect, our ancestors held that there should be no fixed system, laid down by the laws, or set forth by authority, or the same for all.' This was certainly not as a result of any dissatisfaction with the outcome of the State regulation of education in various Greek communities, of which the Romans at this time had little or no knowledge. It was a direct result of the Roman

conception of the unlimited authority of the father (*patria potestas*). As the father had by law the absolute right of regulating the life of the son as he pleased, so he naturally had the entire control of his education. The end of the future citizen's training was recognised to be that he should learn those ' arts '—including both moral qualities and intellectual capacities—which fitted men to be of service to the State (Cicero, *de Rep.* i. 20, 33); and a father was open to grave censure who failed to do his best to secure this. But to lay down in detail which these were, and how they should be acquired, would have been regarded as an encroachment on the sacred sphere of the family, in which the father reigned alone and supreme.

In practice doubtless the charge of the child in its earlier **Duties of the** years fell to the mother. And the Roman matrons, **Mother.** at all events in the better days of the Republic, were not unworthy as a rule to discharge this duty. The position of a wife at Rome was very different from what it was in Greece, especially in the Ionian States. She shared with her husband the rule of the house, and though legally his subordinate, and as much under his control (*in manu eius*) as a daughter, was in her own sphere acknowledged as his equal. The formula used in marriage expressed this clearly : 'Where you are master, I am mistress' (*ubi tu Gaius, ego Gaia*). If she had not by law a *potestas* like that of the father, which in the nature of things could not be divided, yet the *mos maiorum* —the usage of former generations—gave her an authority which in practice may have been hardly less. The character of a woman of the early Republic does not always appear attractive. There is often in it a hardness, a pride in rank, a narrowness and a lack of sympathy, which are not amiable features. On the other hand there is usually a purity, a dignity, a gravity, an industry and a devotion to her family and her country, which fit her to be the head of a household, and to bring up worthy citizens. She rarely discharged duties which were considered menial. Plutarch has a curious discussion in his *Roman*

Questions as to why Roman women did not grind corn or cook in the old days. These were held to be the tasks of slaves. But the *mater familias* would sit in the hall (*atrium*), spinning and weaving with her daughters and her maids, and directing the affairs of the household. So the child was brought up on its mother's knees (*in gremio matris educabatur*). Tacitus tells us (*Dial.* c. 28) that at times some elderly kinswoman of well-approved character was chosen to take care of all the children of one family[1]. This practice, which we are almost surprised to find that Tacitus thinks worthy of mention, can hardly have been very common; but it may have been observed in cases where the children of several sons continued to live under the family roof, or where some hindrance kept the mother from taking the whole charge herself. For the early days of the Republic there is little or no direct evidence as to the attainments of the women, but there is no reason to think that they were inferior to those of the men, and these, as we shall see hereafter, were greater than has often been supposed. We cannot doubt that a Roman mother was, as a rule, well able to give her children at least the rudiments of such education as it was desired that they should receive.

From one of the gravest anxieties of later days she must
Slavery not
extensive.
have been in a great measure free. It has always been one of the most fatal curses of an extensive system of domestic slavery that it tends so much to demoralise the children of the slave-owners. The Romans learnt this, and the best of them lamented over it bitterly, in later days. But in early times the number of slaves at Rome was much smaller. What there were, were either *vernae*, born and bred in the

---

[1] 'Nam pridem suus cuique filius, ex casta parente natus, non in cella emptae nutricis, sed gremio ac sinu matris educabatur, cuiusque praecipua laus erat tueri domum et inservire liberis. Eligebatur autem maior aliqua natu propinqua, cuius probatis spectatisque moribus omnis eiusdem familiae suboles committeretur; coram qua neque dicere fas erat quod turpe dictu, neque facere quod inhonestum factu videretur.'

house, and often the playmates or even the foster-brothers of
their young masters ; or else they were citizens who had fallen
into misfortune, and had been compelled by debt to sacrifice
their freedom.   There were as yet none of those gangs of
barbarous captives, swept off to Rome after one of her victorious
campaigns, there to be treated little better than the brute beasts,
with which they were classed.   Nor were there as yet any of
those troops of household slaves, still more corrupting in their
influence, who later on were the tools of a senseless luxury, and
who under a varnish of culture were familiar with the worst
vices of the East.   The dreams of a Golden Age of simplicity
and purity, in which those love to indulge who are living in the
midst of a complex civilisation, are never so true to history as
the dreamers fancy.   But no doubt it was far easier to train
children to a life of virtue and self-control amid the plainness
and gravity of the early Republic than in the luxurious and
extravagant households of later days.

It is very difficult to say with confidence whether at this
time there were any public schools at Rome.   It
Schools. is true that we find schools referred to in more
than one of the old legends.   Livy for example tells us (iii. 44)
how Verginia was seized as she came down into the Forum,
'for there were schools in the booths there' (*ibi namque in
tabernis litterarum ludi erant*) ; and Dionysius in telling the
same story (xi. 24) gives it the same setting.   Livy has also
something to say about a schoolmaster at Falerii (v. 27), and
he describes (v. 25) how when Camillus entered Tusculum he
found among other signs of profound peace 'the schools resounding with the voices of the scholars.'   But in cases like these,
whatever basis of truth there may be for the stories, it would
be absurd to suppose that Livy, or the source from which he
drew, had any better authority for the details than his own
artistic imagination.   It would be hardly more perilous to draw
an inference, as some have, from the fact that Plutarch tells
us (*Rom.* c. 6) that Romulus and Remus went to school at

Gabii. Indeed apart from the definite statement which assigns the introduction of public schools to a much later date, it is not easy to say what would have been the need for them at this early epoch. When we read of their institution it was because fresh subjects had been brought into education, for which there was no room in the old home-training. But the teaching of the school always supplemented and followed this and did not take its place. So long as no national literature existed, there could be no demand for schools in which it was taught.

Cicero (*de Off.* ii. 46) sums up the qualities which win a **Character-** good reputation for a young man as 'modestia cum **istics desired.** pietate in parentes, in suos benevolentia.' As usual these words mean something rather different from what is suggested by the English words derived from them. We may translate them by 'self-control, accompanied by a dutiful affection to parents, and kindliness towards all the members of one's family.' These are not, it is true, more than 'prima commendatio,' though they form the basis of the ideal character. Fear of the gods and reverence for the laws, temperance and frugality, energy and industry, obedience to authority, courage and patriotism, these and the like were the virtues which the traditional training—the *disciplina maiorum*—aimed at developing in the future citizen, first at his mother's knee, and then at his father's side. The 'mens sana in corpore sano' of later days was the standard from the first, though the meaning of the words may have been somewhat developed afterwards. But the leading feature was restriction and control. 'Life in the case of the Roman,' says Mommsen, 'was spent under conditions of austere restraint, and the nobler he was, the less was he a free man. All-powerful custom restricted him to a narrow range of thought and action: and to have led a serious and strict life, or to use a Latin expression, a grave and severe life, was his glory. Nothing more or less was expected of him than that he should keep his household in good order, and unflinchingly bear his part of counsel and action in public affairs.'

A boy's religious duties were learnt at his father's side.
Religious Education. The essence of early Italian religion did not reside
in the mastery of any body of doctrine as to the
gods or legends about them : still less in cherishing any
emotions of trust or affection towards the unseen powers.
There were certain things which must not be done, just as
there were certain dues which must not be neglected, under
pain of bringing down upon the offender their wrath and the
ensuing punishment. But a faithful discharge of the traditional
observances would secure their favour, and what these observances were it was the duty of each father to teach his son. The
religion of early Rome had its good as well as its bad side. 'It
was a religion for the most part of fear, of multitudinous scruples,
of a year-long burden of forms' (Pater). But at least it kept a
man face to face with his conscience. He knew that the
conduct of his life was a matter to which the powers that
ruled the world were not either blind or indifferent, and that
they would be with him or against him according to his actions.
The Roman's conscience might seem to us in some ways unen-
lightened, but at least he had one and made some attempt to
be guided by it.

For 170 years, says Varro, the Romans worshipped without
an image or a temple. He is counting from the traditional date
of the foundation of the city to the building of the great temple
on the Capitol. No certainty and no importance attaches to
the precise number of years. But it is an important fact that
it was only under foreign influence that the Romans clothed
their deities in human form, and built them habitations to dwell
in. The centre of the devotions of each household was the
family hearth, where they were accustomed every morning to
make offerings to Vesta, goddess of the fire, which was the first
need of the common life as that by which the food was cooked,
to the Penates, the deities who presided over and protected the
store-chamber, and to the Lares, in whom many scholars have
seen the spirits of ancestors, but who were more probably, at

first in the form of the single 'Lar familiaris' but later dupli-
cated, tutelary spirits of the family, and perhaps especially of
the family estate. No religion, says a French scholar, has
created so many deities to protect the house, honoured alike
by the poor and by the rich. Though their attributes are
pretty much the same, one is no hindrance to another; it is
impossible to have too many defenders round the family. Next
to the deities who guarded the home, and hardly second to
them in nearness and importance, were those who protected
the land. When Cato's landholder visits his estate his first
duty is to greet the Lar familiaris, but there are many sacrifices
which he has to pay at the proper season to the gods of the
country. All the various operations of agriculture were com-
menced only after the due prayers and offerings : in the spring
suovetaurilia—a pig, a sheep and a bull—to purify the fields, in
the harvest a *porca praecidanea* to Ceres, twice a year a feast to
Juppiter *dapalis*, sacrifices on behalf of the oxen to Mars Silvanus,
and whenever he had to thin a sacred wood prayers to the
unknown gods who haunted it. But the most imperative of
all was the Ambarvalia, when all work ceased and masters and
slaves went together round the fields, bearing flowers and
incense, and purifying water, and leading the victims that were
shortly to be sacrificed, all moving in reverent silence, while the
priests intoned the archaic and now barely intelligible prayers
to the gods of corn and wine and increase. Perhaps too the
father might be the priest—for at Rome there was no sacer-
dotal caste : the priest was also the farmer, the statesman and
the general, as the call came to him—of some local or national
form of worship ; and then the son would attend him as his
camillus or acolyte, and so learn the traditional ritual, and the
few bald legends connected with it, to hand them on to his
own son in turn, for priesthoods were in most cases hereditary.
A late Latin poet who was a Christian, Prudentius, describes
graphically (*c. Symm.* i. 197–218) how children from their earliest
years were thus familiar with the rites of paganism. The

young heir worshipped whatever his grey-haired ancestors had pointed out as worthy of his reverence; he had seen the hearth and its gods daily honoured with votive perfume; he had watched his mother pale with anxiety praying before the image of Fortune in the house; then he had been lifted on his nurse's shoulders to kiss the statue himself and to put up his childish petitions, and so was imbued with the spirit of his creed long before he marvelled at the splendour of the worship of the Imperial city, and learnt to count all things true which the Senate held as truth. This is said of a much later time; but we need not doubt that what was best in the old Roman religion was due to the home. Indeed until the introduction of the Greek philosophy, with its various systems of reasoned morals—as to which something will have to be said hereafter—there was no religious or moral instruction given anywhere else. Speakers in the Senate or in an assembly of the people might appeal to the laws of right and wrong, or to considerations of religious duty; but this was only because there was a common traditional morality taught in the homes of the people, not because there was any provision for giving formal and authoritative instruction in accordance with it.

The practical duties of citizenship were learnt in the same informal but very effective fashion. The son would receive his first lessons in law, in politics, and in constitutional usages, as he listened to the advice which his father gave from his chair (*solium*) in the hall (*atrium*) early each morning to the clients who came to consult him, or as the elder men talked together at the evening meal over the questions of the day or the great traditions of the past. So it is that as we study Roman history we can often find a hereditary policy pursued by noble families almost as tenaciously as by our own great Whig or Tory houses. Nowhere perhaps, at least in the Western World, has the commemoration of the deeds and the virtues of ancestors played so important a part in education as in Republican Rome. According to a statement, which our authorities ascribe to Cato[1], each guest at a party was expected to sing a song in praise of the heroes of old : 'for this was the special function of the goddesses of song.' Varro (quoted by Nonius, p. 77) puts it somewhat differently : 'assa (*unaccompanied*) voce canebant pueri modesti carmina antiqua, in quibus erant laudes maiorum.' There seems to be no other evidence that Roman boys were at all commonly taught to sing, so that in this form the story is highly doubtful ; and the theory that there was once an extensive literature of rude ballads, which has been based upon the tradition, must unquestionably be rejected[2]. But we may well believe that lessons drawn from the stories of the past supplied the material for much of the moral training of the Roman boy. Even when the father dined abroad, it was usual for his young sons to accompany him, and either at the common table or at small tables of their own to listen to whatever might be discussed. How the reverence always felt to be due to the young tended to check any possible license of speech is shown by the words of old Cato : 'disgraceful language is no less to be avoided when a boy is there, than if the Sacred Virgins were present.' We are told further that the sons of senators were allowed to go with their fathers to the Senate-house, to listen to the discussions there, and so to become early familiar with the policy of the State.

Reading, writing, and such simple calculations as were needed for business purposes were taught by the father, when the mother had ceased to take sole charge[3]; and if it is specially recorded of Cato that he himself taught his son letters, law, and manly exercises, this

Elementary Teaching at Home.

---

[1] Cp. Cic. *Brut.* xix. 75 : 'utinam exstarent illa carmina, quae multis saeculis ante suam aetatem in epulis esse cantitata a singulis convivis de clarorum virorum laudibus in Originibus scriptum reliquit Cato.' Cp. *Tusc.* i. 2, 3: 'est in Originibus solitos esse in epulis canere convivas ad tibicinem de clarorum hominum virtutibus.'

[2] For a criticism of this see Sellar's *Roman Poets of the Republic*.

[3] That the mother did not give up her share of rule in the house,

is rather an instance of his old-fashioned ways than anything which would have been unusual at an earlier time. One reason for his doing so is interesting and significant. He had a slave who was a *litteratus*, and who taught reading and writing to his fellow-slaves, and probably also to many others, so bringing in fees to his owner. 'But Cato thought not fit, as he himself said, to have his son reprimanded by a slave, or pulled, it may be, by the ears when found tardy in his lesson; nor would he have him owe to a servant the obligation of so great a thing as his learning' (Plutarch). He is even said to have written histories in large letters with his own hand, that so his son without stirring out of the house might learn to know about his country-men and forefathers. It may be noted in passing that the physical exercises to which Cato trained his son, were only such as would fit him for service in the army, not for gymnastic competitions. 'Not only did he show him too, how to throw a dart, to fight in armour and to ride, but to box also and to endure both heat and cold, and to swim over the most rapid and rough rivers' (*ib.*). We shall see later on how different this was from the aim and the methods of physical training among the Greeks.

Meanwhile the girls were learning at their mothers' sides
Training
of Girls.
lessons of conduct and the domestic arts. All clothing was at this time made of wool, and the spinning and weaving of this was usually done at home. It is mentioned as a sign of the love—real or affected—of the Emperor Augustus for old-fashioned ways, that he liked to wear a toga, made for him by members of his own family. Whatever teaching in the way of reading and writing was given to boys especially in the country, is evident from such a passage as Hor. *Carm.* iii. 6, 37:

> rusticorum mascula militum
> proles, Sabellis docta ligonibus
>   versare glaebas et severae
>   matris ad arbitrium recisos
> portare fustis.

was doubtless shared equally by the girls ; there are no traces that these attainments were less familiar to the one than to the other sex.

This education, mainly moral and practical, with a very narrow range of intellectual interest, and but little attempt to secure mental culture, was carried on in the case of boys until they changed the dress of boyhood—usually at the age of sixteen or seventeen—for the *toga virilis* or 'garb of manhood, which was the outward sign that they were regarded as fit to begin to take upon themselves the duties of citizenship. But even after the *toga virilis* had been assumed, the supervision and control of parents did not cease, as we find from many curious stories. Of this system of training as a whole Mommsen well says (i. p. 241) : 'This mode of educating youths was in truth one of those institutions of homely and scarce conscious wisdom, which are as simple as they are profound. But amidst the admiration which it awakens we may not overlook the fact that it could only be carried out, and was only carried out, by the sacrifice of true individual culture, and by complete renunciation of the equally charming and perilous gifts of the Muses.'

Defects of the Early Training.

It is just here that we find the crucial difference between Greek and Roman ideals of education. It has been said with truth that the training which made Marathon possible and that which brought Rome out victorious from her long struggle with Hannibal must have had much in common. Undoubtedly they had. It could hardly be otherwise when the aim of both was primarily to train citizens for the service of the State. But as far as we can go back in Greece, alike in Dorian and in Ionian communities, the central element in education is 'music' in the widest sense in which that word was used, including as it did both learning and chanting of songs. But if we compare the general sketch of Greek education put by Plato into the mouth of Protagoras in the dialogue which bears his name, or the description of

Greek and Roman Ideals.

the training of boys in old days given in the *Clouds* of
Aristophanes, with what we have now learnt about the earliest
Roman education, we shall find that the chief difference is just
here. The teaching of good conduct by warning, rebuke and
chastisement takes the first place in all. When in Greece
parents send their sons to teachers 'they enjoin them to see to
his manners even more than to his reading and his music; and
the teachers do as they are desired. But as soon as the boy
has learnt his letters and is beginning to understand what is
written, they put into his hands the works of great poets, which
he reads at school...and these he is required to learn by heart
in order that he may emulate them and desire to become like
them. Then again the teachers of the lyre take similar care
that their young pupil is steady and gets into no mischief, and
when they have taught him the use of the lyre, they introduce
him to other excellent poets, viz. the lyric poets, and they make
their harmonies and rhythms quite familiar to the children, in
order that they may learn to be more gentle and harmonious,
and rhythmical, and so more fitted for speech and action. Then
they send them '—still, be it noticed, away from home—'to the
master of gymnastic, in order that their bodies may better
minister to the virtuous mind, and that the weakness of their
bodies may not force them to play the coward in war or on any
other occasion[1].' So we see that here, just as at Rome, when at
the same stage, the moral improvement of the pupil was the main
thing kept in view; and the contrast in Aristophanes (*Clouds*,
961–1008) between the old and the new ways of studying music
leaves on us the same impression. Only in Greece this aim
was pursued by methods as yet unknown to Rome, because the
necessary material for them was still wanting—methods too
which, tending as they did to a love of culture for its own sake,
led in the long run even in Greece, and still more at Rome, to
a change in the whole spirit of especially the higher education.

---

[1] Plato, *Protag.* p. 325.

It must be also borne in mind that when the Romans first came to feel the full force of the influence of Greece, it was no longer Greece at its best. The lessons which she had to teach were of inestimable value for the spread and developement of culture, but what was best in them was mingled now with the products of a decaying national life. In Mommsen's phrase the enchanter's cup was stale, and the Athens which Rome came to know was no more the Athens of Sophocles and Plato.

CHAPTER III.

EDUCATION UNDER GREEK INFLUENCE.

LIVY tells us (ix. 36) that in early times boys at Rome were trained in Etruscan culture, as they were at a later date in Greek. This statement is so entirely at variance with everything which we know about the nature of Roman education, and not less with all our information as to the range and purpose of Etruscan culture[1], that it is unhesitatingly rejected as incredible by modern scholars. The influences which came to modify so largely the traditional system and methods of education at Rome were entirely of Greek origin. It is impossible to fix a date for the earliest infiltration of Greek culture into Italy. Legends would carry it back to very ancient times; and even putting these aside, we know that before the foundation of Rome Greek colonies had been established in Sicily and Italy. By various channels of trade these had long been extending their influence, as we can see from many traces in the history of the Latin language, at a date much before that of our earliest trustworthy records. But the middle of the third century before Christ, which coincides very nearly with the close of the First Punic

Acquaintance with Greek Culture.

---

[1] This was almost entirely restricted to the art of the *haruspex*, or diviner by means of the vital organs of sacrificial victims, an art which was often employed at Rome, though its professors, who were foreigners, were always despised. The haruspices must be carefully distinguished from the augurs, who were among the most revered of Roman officials, and who held high rank in the State.

War, was marked by a great increase in the inflowing tide of Hellenism.

A certain familiarity with the Greek language, such as would be required by the needs of commerce, must have been widespread among the trading classes. In B.C. 282 Lucius Postumius, the Roman envoy to Tarentum, could address his audience in Greek, though not of the choicest quality; and when Cineas the ambassador of Pyrrhus in the following year addressed the Roman Senate we do not find any mention made of an interpreter (Plutarch, *Pyrrh.* 14). But the best proof of the extent to which Greek was at this time familiar among the upper classes is found in the fact that the earliest Roman historians, Fabius Pictor and Cincius Alimentus, both wrote in Greek, thus showing not only their own command of that language, but also that they could rely upon finding readers among their own countrymen. The keepers of the Sibylline Books must have had a good knowledge of Greek; for these were not only the source from which large additions of a Greek type were made to the Roman ritual, but they were naturally written in Greek (Cicero, *pro Balb.* xxiv. 55). The same is true of the priests of Ceres. For the lower classes it is very significant that the comic poet Plautus (*flor.* 215–185) can always trust a popular audience to take a joke, the point of which turns upon a play on Greek words. To a large proportion of the great and increasing number of imported slaves Greek must have been their native tongue. So we see that a way was already being made for a great change in the aims and methods of education. As a recently discovered fragment of an unknown historian[1] puts it: 'At this time there were

Knowledge of the Greek Language.

---

[1] 'Duae quasi factiones Romae essent, quarum una Graecas artes atque disciplinas adamabat, altera patriae caritatem praetexebat acerrimam' (printed in *Rhein. Mus.* xxxix. 623). In some cases the passion for all that was Greek became quite a mania, and justly called down the ridicule of the satirists of the time.

It is perhaps hard to over-estimate the effect which the ever-growing two parties at Rome, one of which was devoted to the arts and studies of Greece, while the other professed a strong and patriotic attachment to their own country.'

There had long been at Rome a class of teachers—though
Greek Literature. we have no means of knowing how extensively they had been employed—called *litteratores* or writing-masters, mostly either slaves or freedmen. Now there grew up by the side of these a body of *grammatici*, who taught to write and speak Greek. At first doubtless the language was learnt for practical purposes only; there seems to have been no idea of using the literature as an instrument of mental culture. But by degrees, at first perhaps half-unconsciously, the study of the language was extended to include a study of the works written in it. The importance of the step then taken was enormous, for thus the Romans came to be the first nation to base their culture on the study of literature in a foreign language, and so marked out the lines on which the higher education of all civilised nations was to move down to the present time. What Greek was to the Romans, that in its own way Latin was destined to be in the time to come to the nations of Western Europe, and there has never been a time when much of the best training of the mind did not consist in the study of the thought of the past recorded in a language not the student's own. The teachers of Greek, in accordance with the practice usually followed in their own land, had taken as their text-books the works of their greatest authors, and especially the poems of Homer. The *grammatici* would naturally wish to treat the study of the Latin language on the same lines as those on which they had been accustomed to treat the study of the Greek language : and for this the first
Livius Andronicus. thing needed was literary texts. The endeavour to supply these, made by Livius Andronicus about

swarms of household slaves, to many of whom Greek must have been their native language, and who were familiar with Greek life and ways, must have had in Hellenising the upper classes at Rome.

B.C. 250 by translating Homer's Odyssey, was the starting-point of Latin literature. Livius had been a slave and as such had been set to teach the children of his master and of other Roman nobles. After his emancipation he continued his former occupation as a teacher of Greek, but he added to this the study of the great Greek writers in translations. He seems to have chosen the Odyssey rather than the Iliad for translation, thinking that·a poem of adventure would have more attraction for the Romans than one of character; indeed the Iliad did not find a Latin translator before the time of Sulla. He also translated or imitated and brought upon the stage for the first time Greek plays, both tragedies and comedies, and himself took a leading part in acting them. It was for the good service thus rendered by making Greek literature better known to the people at large that the authorities assigned to him the temple of Minerva on the Aventine for the meetings of his 'guild of poets'—*collegium poetarum*—'quia is et scribebat fabulas et agebat' (*Fest.* p. 333). But though his plays were acted with success, they, no less than his Odyssey, were also intended to be used as texts in schools, a purpose which they served at least as late as the boyhood of Horace, nearly two centuries later. The work of Livius was taken up and carried on, with far more poetic talent and much wider learning, by Q. Ennius, the true father of Roman poetry as we know it. (His contemporary Cn. Naevius may well have had more original genius, but he had far less influence over the poets of later generations.)

Suetonius tells us (*de Gramm.* i.)[1] that the modest beginning of the study of literature (which he calls Teaching of *grammatica*) at Rome was when the earliest men Literature.

---

[1] 'Initium quoque eius mediocre exstitit, si quidem antiquissimi doctorum, qui eidem et poetae et semigraeci erant—Livium et Ennium dico, quos utraque lingua domi forisque docuisse adnotatum est—nihil amplius quam‚ Graecos interpretabantur, aut siquid ipsi Latine composuissent praelegebant.'

of learning, who were also both poets and half-Greeks, *i.e.*
Livius and Ennius—of whom it has been recorded that they
taught in each language both at home and abroad—did nothing
but interpret the Greeks, or discourse on anything which they
might have written themselves in Latin.   He goes on to say
that the first in his opinion to introduce the study of 'grammar'
at Rome was Crates of Mallos.   He had been sent by Attalus
of Pergamum as his envoy to the Senate at some time between
the Second (B.C. 202) and the Third (B.C. 149) Punic Wars,
about the time of the death of Ennius (B.C. 169).   By an
accident he broke his leg, and while he was detained at Rome
by this misfortune, he 'gave many lectures and discoursed
diligently, so that he served as a model for the Roman teachers
to imitate.'   But from the very wording of this notice we can
see that what Crates introduced was not more than an improvement in method, though doubtless this may have been of great
value.   Crates was a scholar of the highest reputation, head of
the famous Library of Pergamum, and himself a 'living library.'
Opposed to the Alexandrian school, who laid all stress on the
study of grammar, he contended that the great poets and Homer
in particular could only be understood by the aid of a wide and
comprehensive learning.   This principle was well adapted to
guide the teaching of literature on to those broad lines which
it long continued to follow.   The question has been raised
whether Crates understood Latin.   It is very unlikely that he
did.   The Greeks as a rule were singularly ignorant of all
languages but their own, and despised them as the dialect of
'barbarians,' a contempt which was not without its effect on the
clearness of their own thinking.   But the success of the lectures
of Crates is another proof of the extent to which Greek was
familiar at Rome.   Suetonius goes on to give us the names of
several Romans who made for themselves a reputation as
teachers of literature, and says that afterwards the popularity of
the study and the attention devoted to it grew by degrees, so
much that even men of the highest distinction did not hesitate

to write upon it, and that at one time there were more than twenty famous schools in the city. But this was at a later date, when teaching had become, at least in some cases, a very lucrative profession.

The earliest of the Roman teachers to open a school at which fees were charged was—we are expressly told by Plutarch (*Quaest. Rom.* 59)—one Spurius Carvilius, the freedman of the consul of the same name, who was the first man at Rome to divorce his wife (about B.C. 235–230). The meaning of this statement has been much discussed[1]. It is not in the least likely that all instruction before this had been gratuitous, nor is it probable that there is no foundation for the tradition reported by Plutarch, for which he possibly had very good authority. Perhaps we may think of the teaching as having hitherto been given in private houses, and only to the members of two or three neighbouring families, while Carvilius admitted all who paid his fees. But another explanation seems more in harmony with Roman notions. There was long thought to be something rather discreditable in taking pay for giving instruction. In Greece this feeling contributed largely to the suspicion with which the Sophists were commonly regarded, a feeling which we see reflected in the pages of Plato : the doctrines of many of them had nothing 'sophistical' about them, but they had this in common, that they would not teach except for pay. At Rome legal advice was freely given by the most eminent lawyers to all who desired to consult them. Even in the law-courts advocates were expressly forbidden to receive any fee for their services. Of course in all such cases presents were not prohibited, and in course of time they came to be so usual as to be virtually obligatory. We may think then of

School of Carvilius.

---

[1] One recent writer explains that Carvilius was made consul for his services to education ; another that he divorced his wife. The statement of Plutarch is perfectly clear to any one who will look at the original : (*Quaest. Rom.* 59) πρῶτος ἀνέῳξε γραμματοδιδασκαλεῖον Σπόριος Καρβίλιος, ἀπελεύθερος Καρβιλίου τοῦ πρώτου γαμετὴν ἐκβαλόντος.

Carvilius as substituting for the practice of free-will offerings the payment of fixed fees, or perhaps rather of supplementing the former by the latter. How long the usage of making complimentary presents to teachers lasted will be seen hereafter: there are indeed some curious traces of it in English schools.

There has been some discussion of the question what was taught in a school such as that of Carvilius. Was he a *litterator* simply? *i.e.* one who taught only reading and writing. Or was he the first, or one of the first of the *grammatici*, or teachers of literature? We can hardly feel sure of our answer, seeing that the only passage in which he is mentioned does not state whether he taught Greek as well as Latin. If his instruction was limited to the latter language it is hard to see on what he could have based any literary teaching, except the Laws of the Twelve Tables, a few other laws ascribed to the time of the kings, and perhaps a few hymns, dirges or other religious chants. It is not easy for us to realise a state of things in which there was so widespread a knowledge of reading and writing and yet so little occasion for their use[1]. Mommsen says that the Odyssey of Livius took the place of the laws of the Twelve Tables as a sort of improved primer (iii. 463). This is perhaps going a little too far: for we know that the latter were studied in schools—though not probably as a first lesson-book—down to the time of Cicero. But

Subjects taught by Carvilius.

---

[1] Yet we may remember that even at Athens, where culture was so widespread, there was never anything like a reading public, but literary works came to be known largely by recitation. Cp. Butcher, *Harvard Lectures*, p. 185. The mechanical inconvenience of the papyrus roll doubtless had something to do with checking the free use of books. A freedman in Petronius (c. 58) says: 'I have not learnt any of your mathematics, or aesthetics or nonsense of that kind, but I can read the letters on stones (*lapidarias litteras*), and I can divide by a hundred in money, measures and weights.' These are the *serviles litterae* of which Seneca (*de Tranq. An.* ix. 5) speaks: 'plerisque ignaris etiam servilium litterarum libri non studiorum instrumenta, sed cenationum ornamenta sunt': *i.e.* reading, writing and counting.

certainly from the days of Livius onward translations or imitations of Greek plays and other poems furnished most of the material for teaching in Roman schools.

We must not however suppose that it was only in this
Greek Teachers. indirect way that Greek literature came to be known to the Romans. We have already seen how general, we might almost say universal, the knowledge of the Greek language was among the upper classes, at any rate in the city. The teachers who were inspired by, and learnt the method of Crates, were probably for the most part Greeks, who taught their own language and literature to the young men of Rome. Only we have no reason to believe that as early as the time which we have now in view, Greek had found its way into schools for boys, or held the place in them that it had in later days. Many instances are on record which show how far the mania for all things Greek had gone by the middle of the second century before Christ. We read of the consul of B.C. 131, that when in the province of Asia he could give his decisions not only in the Greek commonly current, but also in any one of the four dialects spoken in that district. This is mentioned as something remarkable, but it points to a high average of attainment.

But meanwhile alongside of, but quite distinct from the study
Rhetoric and Philosophy. of literature in Greek and Latin as a means of general culture, there had come in by degrees something of that training in rhetoric and in philosophy, which had long been regarded as an important part of the higher education in Greece. Doubtless the curriculum of the 'grammar' schools was quite enough for the ordinary citizen; but those who aspired to take a prominent part in public life often wished to train themselves for it by all the resources of Greek culture. We cannot say precisely when this higher teaching was first given at Rome. We are told that in the consulship of Lucius Postumius—which may mean either B.C. 173 or B.C. 155—two Epicurean philosophers Alcius and Philiscus were banished from Rome (Athen. xii. 547, Aelian,

ix. 12), and in B.C. 161 a resolution of the Senate banished the *philosophi et rhetores Latini.* The latter term probably denotes Greeks who used Latin as the medium of their teaching; it is not likely that either philosophy or rhetoric was taught as early as this by native Romans. It was perhaps in order to supply a new demand, which he felt might be otherwise met in a more perilous way by the Greek teachers, that Cato included among the books which he drew up for the training of his son, one on the art of speaking. Two interesting quotations from it have been preserved, which show how far its point of view was removed from that of the sophistical rhetoric, then the bane of the Greek schools. The definition of an orator is: 'vir bonus dicendi peritus.' And the golden rule for oratory is: 'rem tene, verba sequentur.' But it is very significant that in preparing this book Cato, who was the most eloquent speaker of his day, studied carefully the speeches of Demosthenes as well as those found in the pages of Thucydides. So little could the bitterest opponent of Greek culture afford to neglect the resources which it put at his command. The first Roman who seems to have brought a training in formal rhetoric to bear with marked success on public speaking was M. Aemilius Lepidus Porcina (consul in B.C. 137), who was taken as a model by Tiberius and Gaius Gracchus. His style showed careful and effective use of the period, and the polished elegance which comes from the constant use of the pen. His speeches were preserved and were read by Cicero. A somewhat older contemporary Ser. Sulpicius Galba is said by Cicero (*Brut.* 82) 'princeps ex Latinis' to have employed all the arts of rhetoric; but his speeches did not read well, owing to their archaic and un-polished diction, so that he cannot have owed much, at any rate directly, to Greek teachers. On the other hand with Scipio Aemilianus, the son of Aemilius Paulus (p. 36), and his friend Gaius Laelius, who was even more distinguished as an elegant speaker, we are already in the full tide of Greek influence. Both Tiberius and Gaius Gracchus were taught rhetoric by Menelaus

of Marathus and Diophanes of Mitylene ; and we may confidently say that a study of the principles and methods of Greek
rhetoric had become common among the upper classes at
Rome by the middle of the second century B.C. And we need
not doubt that this was of great service in developing the
power and flexibility of the Latin language. Too much
familiarity with Greek culture—whether in rhetoric, in literature or in philosophy—was always looked on with some
suspicion by an average Roman audience in the days of the
Republic ; and Cicero and his contemporaries sometimes amuse
us by their attempts to avoid any display of knowledge[1]. Still
the methods of the Greek rhetoricians were beyond question
very successful in teaching the skilful invention and arrangement of arguments, and a ready command of appropriate
language. Modern critics have often disparaged the value of
their instruction, as dealing only with words ; but the fact
remains, that those politicians to whom the power of effective
speech was of the greatest importance for their success in life—
such men as Cicero and Caesar—were the very men who valued
it the most highly. Rhetoric did not do, what it never professed
to do : it did not teach elevated principles of life, or inspire a
lofty patriotism. But it put into the hands of statesmen, who
aimed at serving their country, a power of persuasion which

---

[1] Cp. Cicero, *de Orat.* ii. 4 : ' Sed hoc fuit in utroque eorum, ut Crassus
non tam existimari vellet non didicisse, quam illa despicere et nostrorum
hominum in omni genere prudentiam Graecis ánteferre : Antonius autem
probabiliorem hoc populo orationem fore censebat suam, si omnino
didicisse nunquam putaretur; atque ita se uterque graviorem fore, si alter
contemnere, alter ne nosse quidem Graecos videretur.' Dr Reid on *pro
Arch.* i. 1 says : ' Roman juries, like some English solicitors, looked on the
literary barrister as unpractical: hence the faltering way in which Cicero
owns to a knowledge of Greek literature in passages like *pro Mur.* 63.'
The feeling lasted long; cp. Tac. *Dial. de Orat.* 2: ' Aper omni eruditione
imbutus contemnebat potius litteras quam nesciebat, tanquam maiorem
industriae et laboris gloriam habiturus si ingenium eius nullis alienarum
artium adminiculis inniti videretur.'

made them better able to do so under the conditions of the time; and if this power was sometimes misused, it was in that only like every other capacity.

The Latin teachers of rhetoric were long viewed with dis-Teaching of trust. In Cicero's boyhood the leading man was a Rhetoric. certain Plotius, who seems to have been a freedman, and, as Seneca says, it was considered discreditable to teach what it was honourable to learn. Cicero himself had been very desirous of studying under Plotius, but had been deterred by the advice of friends, who urged that rhetorical exercises in Greek furnished a better training for the mental faculties. Not long after Plotius, a Roman knight, named Blandus, also began to teach rhetoric at Rome. But in B.C. 92 the two censors—one of whom, L. Licinius Crassus, was the most eloquent and accomplished orator of his day—suppressed the schools in which rhetoric was taught in Latin, as being 'schools of impudence,' and not in keeping with the traditions of older times. Crassus is represented by Cicero (*de Orat.* iii. 24) as defending his action on the ground of the incompetence of the teachers, who were not able to impart any really valuable culture. It is a plausible conjecture that one of the main purposes of Cicero's most finished and original work, the three books *de Oratore*, was to show up the shallowness of the Latin rhetoricians. Undoubtedly the Greek masters had behind them a sound tradition of method, which must have been wanting at first to their Roman imitators; though we shall see later on how the adoption of this by the latter led in the long run to the most marked results, by no means wholly for good, upon education and so upon literature, both in prose and in verse.

It may be noticed in passing that, though rhetoric was no part of the curriculum of the ordinary 'grammar' schools, not a few in the earlier days taught and even wrote upon both literature and rhetoric (Suet. *de Gram.* 4). The tendency of the lower schools to encroach on the sphere of the places of more advanced education, and the 'overlapping' of the training given in the former and of that proper to the latter, which Quintilian regrets in his own day, seems to have begun very early. It will probably last as long as human nature is what it is. (Cp. p. 77.)

Another more serious consequence of the attention paid to
rhetoric may also be noted. It was naturally only
Exclusive
Character studied by those whose position or ambition led
of Higher
Education. them to aim at taking an active part in public life,
and with a view to this at winning distinction in the law-courts or in the popular assembly. Hence the fissure was always widening between the culture open to the mass of the people, and that enjoyed by the upper classes. The earlier education had been meagre and narrow, but at least it had been the same for all; the newer culture was the privilege of a class. The plebeians suspected and disliked what they knew was not for them, and both the training and the literature which resulted from it never wholly lost something of an exclusive and exotic character[1].

Meanwhile an influence hardly less powerful, though even
more strongly resisted, was being exerted by the
Philosophy.
growing attention given to Greek philosophy at
Rome. The study of literature could be taken into the usual school curriculum without awakening any strong opposition. It was not, directly at any rate, in antagonism with traditional ideas of life and conduct ; and put forward no arrogant claims to remould them. But philosophy came forward with its rules for the regulation of life, irrespective of the prescriptions of antiquity. It cannot be too constantly borne in mind that for

---

[1] Cp. Mommsen, *Hist. of Rome*, iii. 439 : 'In education alongside of the simple popular instruction or special training, an exclusive *humanitas* developed itself and eradicated the last remnants of the old social equality'; (p. 444) 'The new idea of "humanity" consisted partly of a more or less superficial appropriation of the aesthetic culture of the Hellenes, partly of privileged Latin culture as an imitation or mutilated copy of the Greek.... Here too we trace the revolution which separated classes and levelled nations.'

thoughtful men in Greece and Rome, philosophy was no idle amusement, but a serious effort to discover that guidance for the conduct of life which the national religion could offer only to a very small extent. If a man wished to know about right and wrong, what he had to do and why he should do it, and was not satisfied with the rules which had been taught him as a child, he would go to a philosopher, never to a priest. Hence even more than rhetoric, philosophy, with its bold questionings of accepted teaching, especially on points of moral conduct, was for many years viewed with grave suspicion at Rome. Although it was by no means the earliest instance of this hostility, yet the famous embassy of B.C. 155 gave occasion for one of the most memorable exhibitions of it. The Athenians had seized Oropus, a town on the borders of Boeotia, which they asserted to be rightfully theirs; and to secure the sanction of the Roman Senate for their action they sent to Rome a deputation of three of the most eminent of the philosophers of their city. Among them was Carneades the founder of the sceptical school known as the New Academy. He, when admitted to an audience by the Senate, pleaded with irresistible force and cleverness the paramount claims of justice, to the great delight of his hearers. But unfortunately on the next day he made an equally brilliant speech to prove that justice was nothing but the right asserted by the stronger. This so horrified the aged Cato, now nearing the close of his active life, that he besought the Senate to settle the business of the embassy as soon as possible, and send them away from the city, for fear they should corrupt the younger generation, by teaching them the art of making right seem wrong and wrong right. But it may be doubted whether the attraction which the brilliant new rhetoric and philosophy, with all its sophistry, had for the younger men did not at least equal the dread and dislike felt for them by men of the old school. Henceforward we find that it was not merely slaves or freedman who taught the sons of the more enlightened Roman nobles. When these had finished such teaching as they could give to their pupils in Greek and Latin literature, there was still a higher stage of culture through which many desired to pass, where the teachers were Greeks of learning, of eminence, and sometimes of considerable wealth. But it must be remembered that this teaching, pursued as it was often till far on into mature life, was purely voluntary, and whether given, as was probably most commonly the case, privately, or in the form of public lectures, formed no part of the regular school education. It was no unusual thing for a Roman noble to have in his house a Greek philosopher as a kind of domestic chaplain; and Cicero, when he had already won distinction in public life, still took lessons in rhetoric and practised declamation, while in later years he himself supervised the practice of younger friends.

It remains to consider the effect of the influx of Greek ideas on the physical training of the young. With the Romans of the early Republic, as with the Spartans in Greece, gymnastic exercises were only encouraged so far as they might help to make men more fit to do service in war. The elaborate training of the athlete, and the strict regulation of his food and drink were thought likely to hinder rather than help him in bearing the hardships of active service. But vigorous bodily exercise was part of the daily life. We find mention of ball-playing of various kinds, the throwing of spears and quoits, swimming, riding, and when occasion offered, hunting, usually on foot with dogs. Varro (apud Non. p. 75) in a passage describing the simplicity of his early life tells us how he never had a saddle to his horse, but always rode bare-back. In the Greek gymnasia the main object was to attain that perfect developement of all the physical powers, which might ensure ease and grace of movement; and the highest honours were bestowed on those athletes at the great national games who did best in the various competitions. To the Roman *gravitas* in the better days it would have seemed unworthy to attach so much importance to what were after all

but amusements, and not pursuits to which a citizen could
properly devote months and years of training. To frequent
gymnasia, as the Greek youths did, was regarded by Romans
of the time of Cicero and even later as likely to lead to
idleness and to the worst kind of immorality (cp. Cic. *de
Rep.* iv. 4: 'Iuventutis vero exercitatio quam absurda in
gymnasiis.' See too *Tusc. Disp.* iv. 70). The complete nudity
usual in the contests of the *palaestra* or wrestling school went
much against the Roman notions of decorum, expressed by
Ennius in the line:

> Flagiti principium est nudare inter cives corpora.

Hence the introduction of Greek exercises at Rome was long
postponed, and bitterly opposed. Such language as that reported by Tacitus (*Ann.* xiv. 20) as used in resisting the
innovation of a festival on Greek lines in honour of Nero, was
doubtless an echo of what had been used with greater effect in
earlier times[1]. Many would have adopted as their own the
language of Seneca (*Ep.* 88, l. 8): 'luctatores et totam oleo ac
luto constantem scientiam expello ex his studiis liberalibus.'
It must not be forgotten however that, though systematic
physical training always formed an essential part of Greek
culture, even as early as Euripides strong warnings were
uttered as to the danger of an undue attention to athletics.
And it may be remembered further that the Romans did not
make the acquaintance of the Greek gymnastics when they

---

[1] 'Ceterum abolitos paulatim patrios mores funditus everti per accitam
licentiam, ut quod usquam corrumpi et corrumpere queat, in urbe visatur,
degeneratque studiis externis iuventus, gymnasia et otia et turpes amores
exercendo...quid superesse nisi ut corpora quoque nudent et caestus
adsumant easque pugnas pro militia et armis meditentur?'

Cp. Lucan, vii. 270: 'Graiis delecta iuventus gymnasiis aderit studio-
que ignava palaestrae, et vix arma ferens.' Plin. *Nat. Hist.* xxxv. 168:
'ceromatis quibus exercendo iuventus nostra corporis vires perdit ani-
morum.' Quintilian (x. 1. 33) contrasts the 'toros athletarum' with the
'militum lacertos.'

formed an integral part of a harmonious and well-devised system of culture, but when they had already degenerated in too many cases into a mere occasion for amusement and display.

Seneca at a later date has some interesting remarks (*Ep.* xv.) on the extent to which the severer athletic exercises are apt to encroach upon the time and strength which should be given to the study of literature or philosophy. They naturally lead to over-eating. Besides, the athlete has to put himself at the orders of the trainers, slaves of low reputation, 'quibus ad votum dies actus est.' Seneca himself advises 'exercitationes et faciles et breves, quae corpus et sine mora lassent et tempori parçant, cuius praecipua ratio habenda est.' Among these he includes running, the use of dumb-bells, jumping, both high and long, and another kind which he calls *saliaris* or, 'ut contumeliosius dicam,' *fullonius*, which seems to have resembled the action of men stamping on clothes in order to wash them. It is somewhat amusing to find Seneca, like the elder Pliny, giving a decided preference to the *gestatio*, or, as it is now humorously called, 'carriage exercise,' for 'it shakes one up and does not hinder study[1],' though he reminds us that it is possible to study even while walking.

No attempt was made to reproduce the Greek athletic festivals at Rome, with competitors of rank and character, before the time of Nero. He built for their use a gymnasium after the Greek model (Tac. *Ann.* xiv. 47; Suet. *Ner.* 12) adjoining his Thermae. Up to this time the gymnasium had been only an appendage to the bath at Rome; whereas in Greece the bath had existed merely as a supplement to the gymnasium. Indeed, as Vitruvius says, *palaestrae* were not *Italicae consuetudinis*.

With gymnastics and with music the Greeks commonly
Dancing.   associated dancing (*orchestike*). This on its introduction at Rome seems to have found both warmer welcome and stronger opposition even than gymnastics.

---

[1] 'Et corpus concutit et studio non officit.'

Evidence of the latter is abundant. Nepos for instance says:
'for we know that according to our views of life music is not
consistent with the character of a leading citizen, while dancing
is actually regarded as a failing, all which with the Greeks is
thought attractive and praiseworthy[1]' (*Epam.* 1). To call a
man a *saltator* was a grievous insult, and to be willing 'saltare
in foro' was a proverbial expression for the greatest shame-
lessness[2]. The disapproval of such an accomplishment was
naturally even stronger in the case of a woman: hence the
well-known judgment passed by Sallust (*Cat.* 25) on Sempronia: 'she played and danced more gracefully than a
virtuous woman need[3].' Horace is in accord with the best
opinion of his own time when he says: 'tenerae nimis mentes
asperioribus formandae studiis' (*Carm.* iii. 24, 52). On the
other hand the very protests against the art show how it was
growing in favour. If Horace complains, 'motus doceri
gaudet Ionicos matura virgo,' we may be sure that he is
describing no imaginary evil. Of the extent to which it was
carried a century before him we have some curious first-hand
evidence. Macrobius in comparing the luxury of his own
time with that of an earlier day quotes from a speech of the
younger Scipio, delivered in B.C. 133, a passage which deserves
to find room here in its original form: 'They are taught
unseemly tricks when they go with dancing boys and a lute
and psaltery to the actors' training school. They learn to
sing songs which our ancestors would have regarded as a
disgrace to free-born lads. Free-born boys and girls, I say,
go to a dancing school with professional dancers. When any
one told me this, I could not get myself to believe that

---

[1] 'Scimus enim musicam nostris moribus abesse ab principis persona,
saltare vero etiam in vitiis poni, quae omnia apud Graecos et grata et laude
digna ducuntur.'

[2] Cp. Cicero, *pro Mur.* 6, 13: 'nemo enim fere saltat sobrius, nisi forte
insanit': *in Pis.* 22 etc.

[3] 'Psallere saltare elegantius quam necesse est probae.'

noblemen taught their children such things: but I was taken to the dancing school, and there upon my word I saw more than fifty boys and girls: among them one—and this made me more sorry for my country than anything—a boy of good family, the son of a candidate for office, not less than twelve years of age, dancing with castanets a dance which a vile slave-boy could not have danced without discredit.' At least three of Cicero's prominent contemporaries prided themselves on their skill in this accomplishment (Macrob. *Sat.* iii. 14). But on the whole Gibbon's remark holds as true of dancing as of music and of the games of the arena: 'the most eminent of the Greeks were actors, the Romans were merely spectators.' And Greek influence never went so far as to raise these pursuits from the rank of mere amusements, and to give them a recognised place in a regular education.

As regards music, which is coupled with dancing in more than one of the quotations above, there was always **Music.** a certain demand for it in the worship of the gods, especially such as were honoured *Graeco ritu.* As early as B.C. 207 we find Livius Andronicus composing a hymn to be sung at a solemn *supplicatio* by twenty-seven Roman maidens, and Horace's *Carmen Saeculare* is a familiar instance of the same kind. But though choruses of boys and maidens are not uncommonly mentioned, there is no reason to think that music took any important place in the education of an ordinary boy or girl. The music-girls who often appear in literature and in works of art as ministering to the pleasure of banqueters, were usually either slaves or freedwomen, and often foreigners. Similarly the guild of flute-players, whose services were essential in the rites of some deities, were professional and salaried performers, of Etruscan origin.

If any one man can be regarded as representing the newer form of education on Greek lines, as old Cato—in **Representatives of Newer Education.** spite of some concessions—represents the training in accordance with the *mos maiorum*, it is

L. Aemilius Paulus, the conqueror of Perseus of Macedon, and the father of the younger Scipio. Plutarch tells us that he devoted himself to the education of his children, whom he not only brought up, as he had been trained himself, in the Roman and ancient discipline, but also and with unusual zeal in that of Greece. To this purpose he not only procured masters to teach them grammar, logic, and rhetoric, but had for them also preceptors in modelling and drawing, managers of horses and dogs, and instructors in field-sports, all from Greece (Plut. *Aem.* 6). It must have been about the year B.C. 167 that Polybius, conversing with Scipio, then eighteen years of age, reminded him of the number of Greek teachers now at Rome, who could give to himself and his brother the instruction for which they were thirsting (Polyb. xxxii. 10, 6). Paulus was the first to bring to Rome a collection of Greek books for use in his own house (Plut. *Aem.* 26), so that the younger Scipio was brought up in the atmosphere of a library. He is even said to have formally invited the Athenians to send him a philosopher to train his children. No wonder that the ' Scipionic circle ' was the source of a steady stream of Hellenising influence. Mommsen (iv. 563) measures the change in the last century of the free Republic by comparing Cato's list of the constituents of general culture with that given by Varro in his *Disciplinarum Libri ix.* The former includes oratory, agriculture, law, war, and medicine ; the subjects treated in Varro's nine books were probably grammar, dialectics, rhetoric, geometry, arithmetic, astronomy, music, medicine and architecture. ' Consequently in the course of this century the sciences of war, jurisprudence and agriculture had been converted from general into professional studies.' It is interesting to notice that the first three on Varro's list, the three earliest introduced into Rome, formed the *trivium* or elementary course in the Middle Ages, while the next four constituted the *quadrivium*, or more advanced course from Martianus Capella onwards.

CHAPTER IV.

ELEMENTARY SCHOOLS AND STUDIES.

Now that we have traced the various stages by which the
Education not National. primitive methods of education at Rome came to
be remoulded on Greek lines, it will be well to
review more systematically the general result. The limits
which naturally suggest themselves are the beginning of the
first century B.C. and the end of the first century A.D. The
former coincides pretty closely with the boyhood of Cicero
(b. 106 B.C.), the latter with the death of Quintilian. During
this time no important changes came about, except such as may
well be noticed in passing, and it will be convenient from the
nature of our authorities to treat the period as a whole. We
shall find many traces still remaining of the old Roman spirit
and aims; but the methods and subjects of education are
broadly speaking those which have been imported along with
the teachers during the preceding century and a half from the
schools of Hellas and especially Athens. It must be noted
however at the outset that our authorities are limited almost
entirely to the training given to boys of the richer classes. We
have only slight and casual references to the education of the
poor. Partly this is due to the effect which a system of slavery
always has in depressing the status of manual labourers, as
comes out clearly enough even with the serfage of the Middle
Ages. There are plenty of instances of 'villeins' rising through

the education given in the monastery or cathedral schools and
in the colleges to high posts in Church and State. But it
is always a question of the elevation of the individual, not of
the class. Partly too, as we have seen already, there was
little in the higher education, as it then was, to appeal to the
needs or tastes of the plebeian. It was intended either as a
training for political life or as an amusement for leisure hours,
and from neither point of view was it of any service to the great
mass of the population. A national education did exist in
a sense in some of the Greek states, if we do not include
the slaves in the nation; there was never anything approaching
it at Rome. Then again we have little or no information as to
the country districts[1]. And even in large towns and the
capital itself, there must have been wide differences among
schools both in fees and in repute. In addition to all this we
must recall how every citizen was left quite free, as we have
seen already, to provide, as his means allowed or his wishes
prescribed, for the teaching of his children. Hence all that we
can do is to sketch out the course of education most usual with
the boys and girls of the more privileged classes, and to
remember that the great bulk of the population, even in Rome
itself, and much more in the rural parts of Italy, had a training
which fell far short of this both in range and in duration.

　　We may notice at the outset that even at this period the
power of the father was so unlimited that he had
the right to determine whether a newborn child
should be reared at all. It is true that like all his
paternal rights, this was not exercised capriciously, or without

The Power of the Father.

---

[1] We get glimpses of one in Petron. c. 46, where Trimalchio describes
how a local schoolmaster who does not know much, but takes great pains,
gives his 'young 'un' (*cicaro*) some teaching during the holidays. The boy
has already learnt the elements of arithmetic ('iam quattuor partes dicit'),
and is clever enough; only he is rather 'gone' on birds ('in aves morbosus
est'). But he has made a good start with Greek, and is very fond of Latin
literature. His patron has bought him some 'rubricated' books (*libra
rubricata*) that he may pick up a little law at home.

the approval of the family *consilium*. Dionysius indeed (ii. 15) ascribes a law to Romulus, forbidding the destruction of any offspring except such as was deformed ; and although the existence of the law may be doubtful, its terms may well express the popular sentiment. Seneca too[1] only says, 'we drown children too, if they are weakly or deformed at birth.' But it is clear that the option of the father went beyond cases such as these. The newborn infant was placed by the nurse at its father's feet, and if he wished it to be reared, he took it up (*suscepit*) and put it back into her arms. Cicero, writing in deep depression (*ad Att.* xi. 9, 3), says, 'utinam susceptus non essem,' where we should say, 'I wish I had never been born.' If the father did not desire the infant, he would turn away, and leave it to the mercy of any chance stranger, who might take it and rear it as a slave. This was the fate of Antonius Gnipho, who was born of free parents in Gaul, 'sed expositus, a nutritore suo manumissus institutusque' (Suet. *de Gramm.* 7 : cp. p. 46). Augustus by virtue of his *patria potestas* forbade the child born of his granddaughter Julia to be reared. A passage from the laws of the Twelve Tables is sometimes adduced to prove this right, but the text is uncertain ; but infanticide was not regarded as a crime until the time of the later Empire, and there was no punishment for it before Constantine.

If the father decided to recognise (*suscipere*) the child, on
Infancy.   the *dies lustricus*, i.e. 'dies quo lustrantur,' which
for boys was the ninth, for girls the eighth after birth, a sacrifice was offered either at home or in some temple, by which the infant was solemnly purified, and a name was given to it. In the case of a boy this would include his personal *praenomen*, the *nomen* of his gens, and the *cognomen* of his family, *e.g.* Publius Cornelius Scipio, whereas a girl would only have the gentile name in the feminine form and sometimes her father's cognomen in the genitive, *e.g.* Cornelia Scipionis.

---

[1] *de Ira*, i. 15: 'liberos quoque, si debiles monstrosique editi sunt, mergimus.' Christian apologists pride themselves on their condemnation of the exposure of children. Cp. Athenag. *Leg.* 34.

Sometimes for convenience the girls were numbered.   From
this name-day onwards children wore round their necks a kind
of locket (*bulla*), among the richer classes made of gold, with
the poor of leather, which was supposed to preserve them from
the 'overlooking' (*fascinatio*) of the evil eye.   To wear this was
a sign of free birth (*ingenuitas*).   Wet-nurses were very commonly
employed, and the energy with which philosophers tried to
impress upon mothers the importance of discharging their
natural duties is the best evidence of the extent to which they
were avoided.   But in good families the *nutrices* were chosen
with care, and their names often appear on sepulchral inscriptions.   Many scenes of child-life depicted on sarcophagi and
other works of art give pleasing evidence of the interest taken
by parents in the daily occupations of their children.   Games
and toys of many kinds were plentiful[1]; one monument has
preserved to us a curious representation of a kind of go-cart,
in which a child is learning to walk.   Greek nurses were often
preferred because of their superior intelligence, and great
pains were taken by careful mothers to see that the children
should learn from them only correct speech and refined
pronunciation.

But boys soon passed out of the care of women slaves into
that of men.   It had long been the custom in
Greece for boys to be placed under the charge of
slave-tutors, called *paedagogi*.   It was not the duty of these
men to give instruction, except perhaps in quite the elements
of education.   But they had to look after the manners and
morals of their charges, and in particular to guide them safely
to and from the schools.   Plato says (*Laws*, vii. p. 808) that

Paedagogi.

---

[1] We happen to have much fuller details as to the games played in
Greece than of those in favour at Rome; but Roman children, like ours,
built houses, drove carts, rode hobby-horses, played with dolls, threw
stones to skim the surface of the water, whipped tops, used stilts, and, what
was considered effeminate in a big boy, drove a hoop (*trochus*) with a
clavis adunca.   Marquardt, *Privatalt.* p. 837, where many references are
given.

sheep can no more live without a shepherd than boys without a paedagogus. When at Rome boys began to be sent to be taught in the *ludi* instead of learning at home, a similar class of slaves became a necessity. The name was not always the same. Sometimes the word was *pedisequus*, 'attendant,' sometimes *comes*, 'companion,' or *rector*, 'governor'; most commonly perhaps *custos*, 'guardian.' But even as early as Plautus (*Bacch.* 433 ; *Pseud.* 477) and Terence (*Phorm.* 144) we find the Greek word in use. The former is indeed probably mixing up Greek and Roman customs after his usual fashion, and the latter humorously applies the term to a young lover who dances attendance on the object of his devotion, as she goes on her way to and from school. But soon it came to be the recognised term, and we find it regularly in use under the Empire. It is very often used in inscriptions, and it is quite regular in Quintilian. Suetonius tells us (*Oct.* 44) how Augustus set apart one block of seats in the theatre for 'praetextati,' *i.e.* boys of good birth, and 'proximum paedagogis,' *i.e.* the next block for the slaves in attendance on them. Of course these paedagogi differed very widely in character. Being charged especially with the oversight of the manners and conduct of the children, they should have been chosen mainly with a view to their own morals, but too often they were simply assigned to these duties, when age or ill-health unfitted them for other work, as was not seldom the case with teachers of the poor in much later days. Nor was their moral character by any means always free from reproach. As to their intellectual qualifications Quintilian (i. 1, 8) has a shrewd remark. He says that they should either be sound scholars, or should know that they are not scholars at all ; otherwise they are apt to be assuming and overbearing, and to teach nothing but their own folly. In short for them 'a little learning is a dangerous thing.'

The duties of a paedagogus commonly began when a child was seven years of age. In a wealthy house each child would have one assigned to him, girls as well as boys. At Rome the paedagogus was not so strictly limited to the work of supervision

as was usual in Greece : he would generally at least teach how
to talk Greek, which in many cases would be his native language.
Varro (Non. p. 477) defines his duties in a well-known saying :
'educit obstetrix, educat nutrix, instituit paedagogus, docet
magister.' And though the *institutio* was mainly moral, there
was doubtless enough elementary teaching given to explain
such a use of the term as we find in St Paul's Epistle to the
Galatians (iii. 25). It is tempting there, but probably not
correct, to understand the term of the attendant slave, who
escorted the pupil to the school of the true teacher (cp. Light-
foot's note *ad loc.*). Sometimes, but less commonly, an old
female slave acted as the paedagogus of a girl (cp. *Corp. Inscr.
Lat.* vi. 6331 ; but see also 6330, 6627).

It is probable that in the wealthier families the elementary

The Schools. instruction was usually given at home, either by an
educated slave or by a visiting *litterator*. The very
interesting discussion in Quintilian (i. 2) as to the comparative
advantages of teaching at home and at school deals with a
stage slightly more advanced. But of course for the middle
and the poorer classes going to school would be the rule from
the first. It is curiously difficult to determine whether the
ordinary schools were attended by girls as well as boys. Some
good modern authorities assert confidently that they were[1] ;
but the evidence is by no means convincing. Some of the
passages adduced only show that girls had instruction of the
same kind as boys, and profited by it, as when Sallust (*Cat.* 25)
tells us that Sempronia was well trained in Greek and Latin
literature, or when Pliny says the same thing of Fundania
(*Ep.* v. 16); but this is not disputed. The language of Horace[2]
only shows that eminent musicians had female pupils. Suetonius
tells us (*de Gramm.* 16) that a freedman of Atticus, when
teaching a daughter of his patron, was suspected of betraying

---

[1] Cp. Friedlaender, *Sittengeschichte*, i. p. 457, ed. 6 ; Marquardt,
Privatalt. p. 110; and on the other hand Jullien, *Les Professeurs de
Littérature dans l'ancienne Rome*, pp. 147 ff.

[2] *Sat.* i. 10, 99: 'discipularum inter iubeo plorare cathedras.'

his trust and was dismissed ; but this certainly refers to private tuition. Two passages have been quoted from Martial to prove the point. In viii. 3, 13 the poet asks if he is to write tragedies or epics,

> praelegat ut tumidus rauca te voce magister,
>   oderit et grandis virgo bonusque puer.

This of course may only mean 'school-boys and school-girls alike,' not necessarily in the same classes. So in *Ep.* ix. 68, 2, where a schoolmaster is called 'invisum pueris virginibusque caput,' it may mean 'hated by boys and girls alike, whichever he happens to be teaching.' There is a tombstone found at Capua of an old schoolmaster, representing him with a boy on one side and a girl on the other[1] ; and in the regulations for the educational endowments at Teos[2] it is provided that the professors of literature should teach both boys and girls. Still these facts do not give trustworthy evidence for the practice at Rome ; and if mixed classes had been the rule, we should probably have had clearer proof that it was so. Perhaps we may best regard the practice of 'co-education' as usual in country places, where its advantages are obvious, and quite the exception in the capital, where it would be much less necessary. But even in the country most of the parents who cared to give their daughters anything in the way of a higher education, would be able to provide this, at least in its earlier stages, either themselves or through slaves who had enjoyed some culture. In any case we may assume that even in families where the boys were sent at the age of seven or thereabouts to begin their elementary teaching at school, the girls began it at home.

The regular term for a school was *ludus*, a name chosen

Buildings used for Schools. —so the grammarian Festus (p. 347) assures us— lest by using some more deterrent word attendance should be discouraged[3]. In just the same way 'scholae dictae sunt ex Graeco (σχολή, 'leisure'), non ab otio

---

[1] *Hermes* i. 147.   [2] *Hermes* ix. 502.
[3] Cp. p. 122 : 'sic ludum dicimus, in quo minime luditur.'

et vacatione omni, sed quod, ceteris rebus omissis, vacare liberalibus studiis pueri debent.' But even in Cicero *schola* always retains the meaning either of philosophical discussion, or of lecture-hall where such a discussion was held or higher education given. It would be difficult to find a passage in classical Latin, in which *schola* is used of an elementary school. We read that the school was commonly held *in pergula*. This word is used in somewhat various senses. But it generally denotes a kind of veranda, with a roof but open at the sides. Sometimes it was much the same as a *taberna* or open shop, such as those which still cluster round large houses and public buildings in Italian towns, or those of which there are abundant examples at Pompeii. Sometimes the *pergula* is a kind of loggia on the roof (Suet. *Aug.* 94), sometimes a trellis-covered walk. But we may think of the *pergula* used for teaching purposes as being ordinarily a room on the ground-floor, open to the street in front, and often on the sides as well. Some of the scenes of school-life preserved to us in the frescoes of Pompeii (cp. Helbig, *Wandg. Camp.*, Nos. 1492, 1499) are evidently in the open air or only under cover of a roof. The Italians of to-day still carry on trades and professions in places in full view of the public, to an extent which surprises a stranger from the North. At a later date *pergulae magistrales* came to be the regular term for the lecture-rooms of the rhetoricians (cp. Hist. Aug. *Sat.* 10). To judge from a passage in St Augustine (*Conf.* i. 13) curtains were sometimes used to separate the *pergula* from the street.

The head teacher sat on his *cathedra*, a chair with a round

Furniture of Schools.

back, generally raised on a platform (*pulpitum*). If there was an assistant teacher he would sit on a *sella*, which was placed on the floor and had no back. The pupils sat on wooden benches, so that Seneca says 'apud Sotionem sedi' (*Ep.* 42, 32) for ' I attended the classes of Sotion.' But pupils rose to recite, whether it was a passage which they had learned by heart, or one of their own composition. In writing they commonly rested their tablets on their knees; we do not read of tables or desks, nor do we see any such furniture represented.

The better class of schools were often adorned after the Greek fashion with busts of famous authors or other portraits. There is probably a reference to this in Juvenal (vii. 226):

> Cum totus decolor esset
> Flaccus et haereret nigro fuligo Maroni.

But Mr Duff here prefers to follow the scholiast, and to understand the references to be to copies of the works of Horace and Vergil. The walls were also adorned with tablets containing pictures, incised on marble or on plaster, of scenes from mythology or history; the most famous of these, though by no means the only one preserved to us more or less complete, is the Tabula Iliaca, now in the Capitoline Museum at Rome. The inscription on it makes it clear that it was intended to teach pupils in schools the main incidents in the Trojan War (cp. *Corp. Inscr. Graec.* iii. 844). There is some reason for thinking that this particular tablet was used to aid the studies of young Octavius—afterwards Augustus—and that it was preserved as a memorial of him. Maps were in existence, but there is no evidence that they were used in schools; nor indeed does geography appear to have been studied until a later date. Eumenius says[1] (*de Restaur. Schol.* 120), 'Let the boys also see in these cloisters and daily have before their eyes all the lands and seas, all the towns and nations and tribes, which our victorious emperors subdue. For thus to illuminate youth, that by means of the eyes things may be learnt, which otherwise are grasped with more difficulty, the position, the extent, the distances of all are given along with

[1] 'Videat iuventus praeterea in illis porticibus et quotidie spectet omnes terras et cuncta maria et quidquid invictissimi principes urbium, gentium, nationum...devincunt. Siquidem illic...illustrandae pueritiae causa, quo manifestius oculis discerentur, quae difficilius percipiuntur omnium cum nominibus suis locorum situs, spatia, intervalla descripta sunt.'

their names.' But this dates from Gaul in the fourth century after Christ; and the reference in St Jerome (*Ep.* 60, 7) to the use of maps is not earlier. But. Propertius (v. 3, 37), 'cogor et a tabula pictos ediscere mundos,' proves the use of maps in private houses; and Varro (*de Re Rust.* 1, 2, 1) has a reference to a 'picta Italia' on the walls of a temple.

The social position of the teachers seems to have varied **Emoluments of Teachers.** greatly, but seeing that any one could open a school without any regular license, and that the attainments needed for the early stages of instruction were very slight, we may well believe that it was in most cases but humble. As to the fees, the only definite evidence which we have refers not to Rome, but to a third-rate school in a country town. Horace tells us (*Sat.* i. 6, 76) that his father did not care to send him where the sons of his neighbours went, taking eight *asses* (i.e. about 4*d.*) each month as their fee. Even allowing for the much higher purchasing power of money in those days—not less than three times what it is at present in the case of necessaries—this cannot have amounted to more than about a shilling a month. There were, it is true, certain customary presents, like those which formed a not inconsiderable part of the emoluments of some of our masters of grammar-schools down to recent times. On the Kalends of January, on the festivals of Minerva, of Saturn, of Cara Cognatio, of the Septimontium and on other occasions, it was usual for pupils to bring their offerings. And we shall hereafter come across instances in which popular or fortunate professors of literature were in receipt of handsome incomes. But there is no reason to doubt that the complaints of the less successful, as we find them reported for example by Juvenal, were often well founded. Suetonius tells us of one distinguished teacher of literature of the time of Cicero, M. Antonius Gnipho, that he never would make any stipulation as to his fees : 'nec unquam de mercedibus pactus, eoque plura ex liberalitate discentium consecutus.' But he belonged to a much higher class of teachers than those whom we are at present considering. We find some instances in which the father contracts to pay an annual sum for his son's tuition, but the monthly payment of fees was certainly the more usual practice[1].

There has been much discussion as to the length of the holidays. It has often been assumed that they

Holidays. extended over four months of the summer continuously, in addition to the many incidental holidays. This view mainly rested on a false reading of the line of Horace referred to above. Some editors used to read 'pueri...ibant octonis referentes Idibus aera'; and then this reading was by some —not by all—interpreted to mean that boys went to this school taking their fees on eight of the twelve Ides each year. But there is now no doubt that the true reading is 'octonos referentes Idibus aeris,' and that we may learn from it (as we have seen above) the fee paid, not the number of months in which it was due. Martial (x. 62) bids the *ludi magister* to allow his instruments of punishment to have a rest till the Ides of October, for 'if boys keep well in the summer they are learning enough[2]': but he does not evidently mean that he is to close his school altogether—if this had been the practice, as some have assumed, the poet's advice would have been needless —but only that, like wise teachers nowadays, he should not press his pupils when the weather was extremely hot. There is therefore no real evidence for a four months' vacation in the summer, though there was no doubt a good respite in the hottest season, when all who could left Rome for the country. We may assume too that there was little or no attendance at school during the harvest or the vintage. There were certainly shorter

---

[1] One of the arguments used by Macrobius (i. 12) to prove that March was once the first month of the year runs as follows: 'hoc mense mercedes exsolvebant magistris, quas completus annus deberi fecit.' Whatever we may think of the argument, Macrobius is good authority for the fact.

[2] 'Aestate pueri si valent, satis discunt.'

holidays in December at the Saturnalia—which were in practice celebrated for seven days, though the religious festival was only on one day, and the legal holiday only extended over three, or after the time of Gaius over five—and in March at the Quinquatrus, originally for one but afterwards for five days. Further we cannot doubt that at all events the greater public festivals were kept as holidays in schools; and Mommsen has estimated that the seven more important fixed festivals alone took up 62 days every year, to say nothing of the minor feasts, or of extraordinary gladiatorial shows or other games. Varro, quoted by Nonius, p. 214, says that boys 'exspectant nundinas, ut magister dimittat lusum.' Hence it appears that the *nundinae*, which came every eighth day, and on which the farmers were accustomed to bring their produce to market, were observed, at least in part, as holidays.

The school day began betimes. Ovid tells (*Am.* i. 13, 17)
School Hours. how dawn robs children of their sleep, and hands them over to the schoolmasters, with the canings for their tender hands. Martial (ix. 69, 3) describes how even before cock-crow the streets are resounding with the angry voice and the blows of the master, and (xii. 75, 5) how this spoils all chance of sleep in the early morning hours. Juvenal (vii. 223) represents it as one of the hardships of a teacher's life that he has to breathe air in his schoolroom poisoned by the smoke of the many lanterns which the pupils brought before dawn. Ausonius at a somewhat later date speaks (*Epist.* x. 18, 10) of six hours as the usual length of the school day. But the curious *Colloquia Scholastica*—dialogues in Greek and Latin of an uncertain date[1]—describes how the pupils go off

---

[1] The *Colloquia* were printed in the collection of glossaries made by H. Stephanus, and are reprinted in the London edition of his *Thesaurus Linguae Graecae* (1816). They have sometimes been regarded as an anticipation of the Bell-Lancaster system of mutual instruction, but they are more probably intended to teach Latin to Greek boys. Cp. Bernhardy, *Roem. Litt.* p. 93.

in the middle of the morning to their homes to get their breakfast and to change their dress. Often however boys bought cakes on their way to school, as a light early breakfast[1]. Boys of good position were followed to school not only by the *paedagogus* but also by a *capsarius*, a slave whose duty it was to carry the *capsa*, a cylindrical box containing the rolls of books needed for study, and the tablets for writing on. Poorer boys would naturally carry these for themselves, 'laevo suspensi loculos tabulamque lacerto' (Hor. *Ep*. i. 1, 56).

Discipline was undoubtedly severe. The hot temper of the schoolmaster was almost proverbial, not always to be defended by Cicero's quaint and dubious excuse (*pro Rosc. Com*. 11, 31), 'quo quisque est sollertior et ingeniosior, hoc docet iracundius et laboriosius; quod enim ipse celeriter arripuit, id cum tarde percipi videt, discruciatur.' Seneca (*Ep*. 94, 9) speaks of the inconsistency when 'irascendum non esse magister iracundissimus disputat.' The 'sceptre of the pedagogues,' as Martial calls it, was the *ferula* or rod, usually the stalk of the *ferula communis* or *narthex* (cp. Isidor. *Orig*. xvii. 9: 'a feriendo ferulam dicunt, hac enim pueri vapulare solent'). It was commonly applied to the hand: Juvenal's phrase (i. 15), 'et nos ergo manum ferulae subduximus,' means therefore 'I too then have had my share of caning at school.' Ovid represents Achilles as fearing the same punishment from the Centaur Chiron (*Art. Am*. i. 15: 'poscente magistro verberibus iussas praebuit ille manus'). So too Juv. vii. 210: 'metuens virgae iam grandis Achilles.' But the *ferula* was only used for slighter offences. For graver faults the instrument of punishment was the *scutica* or whip with one or more thongs of leather. The manner in which this was used is shown in a fresco found at Herculaneum (*Pitt. Ercol*. iii. 41) and frequently reproduced, which represents a pupil 'horsed' by another, while a third holds his feet, and the master administers a flogging on his bare back. (In this case how-

Punishments.

---

[1] Cp. Mart. xiv. 223: 'iam vendit pueris ientacula pistor.'

ever the instrument of punishment looks more like the *ferula* or *virga.*) The scourge (*flagellum*) seems only to have been used for slaves ; there is no evidence that so terrible an implement of torture ever found a place in schools.

The question has been raised whether corporal punishment was not limited to elementary schools. It would be difficult to prove that this was the case ; and there is some evidence to the contrary. Orbilius, for example, the teacher of Horace at Rome, to whom he has attached such an unenviable reputation by his epithet *plagosus*, was certainly not a mere *ludi magister.* And he 'ferula scuticaque cecidit' (Domit. Mars. ap. Sueton. *de Gramm.* 9). It is quite the exception to find any one protesting against the use of the cane, as Quintilian did (i. 3, 14), giving excellent reasons for his views. The great majority would probably have agreed with the doctrine put forward so frankly by Ausonius in his 'protrepticon' (exhortation) to his grandson (*Idyll.* iv.), that he must not mind the severe discipline of school, for that is what made his father and his mother what they are. In this respect the Greek practice did not differ from the Roman. The well-known line of Menander, 'the man who has not been flogged is not trained' (*Sent.* 422), may perhaps be only figurative ; but Chrysippus, the famous Stoic, definitely defended corporal chastisement[1]. A stern and even cruel discipline was by no means out of keeping with the Roman character, but it may well have been in part one of those demoralising results which a system of slavery always brings in its train.

It was a common view that children should have nothing to do with the literary side of education before they were seven years of age. But Quintilian agrees rather with Chrysippus[2], who argued that even before the child had left the nurse's care, the training

Age of beginning School-work.

---

[1] Cp. Quintilian (*l. c.*), 'caedi vero discentes quanquam et receptum sit et Chrysippus non improbet minime velim.'

[2] Erasmus quotes Chrysippus with approval at the beginning of his Treatise, *De Pueris statim instituendis.* See Woodward's *Erasmus and*

ought to have begun. One of his arguments is still often heard. He admits that the child will not make so much progress during three or four years at this stage as during one year later on. Still why should such gain as is possible before the age of seven be despised? If the child has got over his rudiments by that time, he will be able then to go on to something more difficult. Children must be doing something as soon as they can talk, and why should they not be doing something which will be of use to them afterwards? Besides, it is a good thing that they should be removed betimes from the influence of slaves, and of frivolous mothers. However, at this stage he would use no pressure, for fear that the pupil, who cannot yet love study, should learn to hate it. He would make it as much as possible an amusement and a privilege, and approves of the common practice of giving children ivory letters to play with : ' et si quid aliud, quo magis illa aetas gaudeat, inveniri potest, quod tractare, intueri, nominare iucundum sit[1].'

Quintilian does not think it below his dignity to give his advice on the most elementary stages. He does not approve of the common practice that children should learn the names and the order of the letters before their shapes. This really hinders the child from recognising them when arranged in a different order. Reading and writing are learnt side by side. As soon as the child can follow the lines of the letters, he recommends the use of a kind of stencil, so that the letters may be traced, without the guidance of the master's hand, which seems to have been usual. Quintilian here does not lose the chance of enlarging on the advantage, especially for a literary man, of a rapid and legible

Methods of teaching the Elements.

Education, pp. 179–222 for the text of this tract, which indeed is largely an application of Quintilian to the German world of Erasmus' day.

[1] The familiar lines of Horace (*Sat.* i. 1, 25), 'pueris olim dant crustula blandi doctores elementa velint ut discere prima,' perhaps refer to the teaching of home rather than the school. Jerome (*Ep.* 12) recommends the same method for the earliest training of Pacatula.

handwriting, 'quae fere ab honestis neglegi solet.' Whereas in Greece the 'letter-method' of learning to read was usual, at Rome the syllabic method was commonly adopted. For this, Quintilian says, there is no short cut; all must be thoroughly learnt, and not the more difficult postponed. The syllables must be read very slowly until they are perfectly familiar, and can be read without hesitation.

When once the letters had been learnt, further teaching was given both in reading and in writing by means of the *dictata magistri*, moral sentiments, like our copy-book maxims, dictated by the master[1]. Under the Republic books seem to have been scarce and costly until the establishment of large organisations of copying slaves, such as that which belonged to Atticus, the friend of Cicero. By means of these books were produced so abundantly that under the Empire they were quite cheap and plentiful. Martial tells us that the First Book of his Epigrams would cost in its most elegant form about three shillings (i. 117), but he also says that the bookseller could make a profit by selling another book of his, the Xenia, covering about 16 pages, for less than four pence[2]. So every school-boy may well have had his own text-books consisting mainly, no doubt, of the standard poets, and from these he may have learnt to read long before he began to study them critically. Great stress was laid upon the importance of a clear and correct pronunciation. If we may trust the *Colloquia scholastica* an older pupil had to pronounce each word as well as the master, and the younger ones had to imitate him. The same authority tells us that the pupils sometimes dictated to each other. In any case we may well believe

Text-books.

---

[1] For this purpose the lines of Publilius Syrus were well adapted and often used. Jerome (*ad Lact.* 107) quotes a verse with the remark ' legi quondam in scholis puer.' Cp. Phaedr. iii. *Epit.* 33: ' ego quondam legi quam puer sententiam : palam muttire plebeis piaculum est.'

[2] Friedlaender, *Sittengeschichte Roms*, iii. 417, has collected a number of interesting examples of the rapid multiplication and dissemination of literature by means of written copies.

that the old precept was observed : 'multum legendum esse, non multa' (Plin. *Ep.* vii. 9).

Writing, as we have seen, was commonly taught by guiding the hand of the pupil over letters already traced on a wax tablet ('litteras praeformatas persequi,' Quint. v. 14, 31), as had been usual in Greece (Plato, *Prot.* p. 326 D). So Seneca says: 'digiti puerorum tenentur et aliena manu per litterarum simulacra ducuntur ; deinde iubentur imitari proposita et ad illa reformare chirographum' (*Ep.* 94, 51). Paper was rarely used, at any rate under the Republic, except for the rolls which were the ordinary form for books at this time :—books like ours with leaves of parchment (*codices* or *membranae*) were not common till the end of the first century A.D. :—but the backs of spoiled sheets of papyrus were used as scribbling paper in the schools (Mart. iv. 86, 11 : 'inversa pueris arande charta'). Parchment, as admitting of being easily cleaned, was sometimes used for rough notes or a first draft, but as a rule writing in schools was done with the *stilus* on a wax tablet (*cera*).

The Roman system of numerical notation, which was very

Arithmetic. cumbrous[1], made the study of arithmetic far from easy : we find that boys carried on their training in this later than in other elementary subjects (Isidor. *Orig.* i. 3, 1 : 'Primordia grammaticae artis litterae communes existunt, quas librarii et calculatores sequuntur'), and the teachers received higher fees (Aug. *Conf.* i. 13, 22). In some cases the teaching of arithmetic seems to have been given in a high school (Bede, p. 72). We have still preserved to us elaborate accounts of the manner in which the fingers were used for calculation[2]. An orator was expected, according to Quintilian (i. 10, 35), not only to be able to make his calculations in court, but also to show clearly to his audience how he arrived at his results. For more

---

[1] The decimal basis of notation necessarily presents great difficulties in calculations involving division by 3, or any multiple thereof.

[2] Cp. Cic. *ad Att.* v. 21 : 'hoc quid intersit, si tuos digitos novi, certe habes subductum.'

elaborate calculations an *abacus* was employed. One kind was quite simple. In this pebbles (*calculi*) were used, and any operation of addition or subtraction could easily be performed, provided the numbers were not too large. When this was the case it was necessary to mark the board out by lines, so that pebbles placed on these had a conventional value. There was one line for units, one for fives, one for tens, one for fifties, one for hundreds, one for five hundreds, and one for thousands. On such boards not only larger sums could be dealt with, but it was possible to multiply and divide. Another kind of abacus, of which several specimens have been preserved, was worked by means of sliding knobs, moving in sunken channels, of which eight shorter ones, each furnished with one knob, face eight longer ones, each provided with four knobs. The details of the working are rather complicated, but the general principle is the same as in the simpler kind, the value of each sign depending on its position, according as the mark was I, V, X, L, C, D, M.

Quintilian brings out the importance attached to arithmetic, when he says (i. 10, 35), 'numerorum quidem notitia non oratori modo, sed cuicunque saltem primis litteris erudito necessaria est.' There was a special class of teachers called *calculatores* (cp. Martial x. 62), but it is not certain whether they had schools of their own or taught in the ordinary elementary schools[1]. Probably there were instances of both arrangements. At all events it is not likely that the great bulk of the children, whose circumstances did not allow them to proceed to the higher schools, were left without a thorough training in so useful and much valued a branch of knowledge. Of course this does not exclude the probability that many children, both boys and girls, may have had lessons at home from special teachers. Perhaps the scene sketched by Horace in *Art. Poet.* v. 325 points to something of the kind. Augustine tells us (*Conf.* i. 13) how

---

[1] The analogy of the 'Writing Master' and the 'Writing School' in English education of the 17th and 18th centuries may be noted.

'unum et unum duo, et duo quatuor, odiosa cantio erat'; and how 'illas primas ubi legere et scribere discitur [litteras], non minus onerosas poenalesque habebam, quam omnes Graecas.' But he was passionately fond of the Latin literature, 'non quas prima magistri, sed quas docent qui grammatici vocantur.'

It is probable that for the great bulk of the population
Schools of education ceased when the elementary school was
Literature. left. There was nothing answering to our technical or commercial education, except what might be given by a father to his sons in his workshop or place of business. As for the girls of the poorer classes, household duties would soon claim them, and they married early. Twelve was the legal and in practice by no means an unusual age, and fourteen may perhaps be taken as the average[1]. Quintilian's wife died before she was nineteen, leaving behind two sons, who were not twins. But the regular course for all who could afford it was to proceed from the elementary teaching of the *litterator* to the higher instruction of the *grammaticus* (cp. Apul. *Flor.* 20: 'prima cratera litteratoris ruditatem eximit, secunda grammatici doctrina instruit, tertia rhetoris armat'). Here the basis of the teaching was the study of literature. It has been well observed that on the one hand there was the greatest freedom left to the master; there was no prescribed curriculum, no impending examination, no State interference in any way. On the other hand there seems to have been in practice remarkable uniformity both in the ideals and in the methods. This was due mainly to the fact that the teachers, if not Greeks themselves, had been trained by Greeks and followed on the lines which had been approved in the Greek schools. To this however there was one important and remarkable exception. In the Greek schools no literature had ever been studied except what was written in their own language. Of course

[1] Cp. Friedlaender, *Sittengesch. Roms*, i. 563–574, who bases his statement on a large collection of facts drawn both from literary sources and from inscriptions.

different dialects were used for different kinds of poetry, and thus some place was made for linguistic studies. But the Greeks never had to deal with thought expressed in a medium with which they were not familiar ; and the history of the Greek intellect shows not a few limitations which may be directly traced to this. But when a Roman boy passed on to the study of literature, it was a question whether he should first take up literature in Greek or in Latin. Quintilian (i. 1, 12), rather to our surprise, decides in favour of Greek. He says that a boy will pick up his Latin, the language of the majority, —a phrase which throws some light on the prevalence of Greek at Rome—even against our will ; besides the Greek methods are the source of the Latin, and therefore should be studied first. Not however that boys should be kept long exclusively to Greek ; otherwise they will fall into bad habits, both of pronunciation and of idiom. Latin should shortly follow and be studied alongside. Quintilian is perhaps speaking here rather of the elementary school, but his arguments would hold good for the school of literature. Sometimes there were different teachers for the two languages (*grammatici Graeci* and *Latini*[1]) and perhaps even different schools, but it was not uncommon for the same man to teach both. In any case the methods were the same (Quint. i. 4, 1), as indeed was natural, seeing that the Latin schools simply transferred to their own literature the methods and principles which they had learnt as applied to Greek. Whether prose was studied at all is open to question ; the evidence is not clear and has been variously interpreted[2], but it is certain that by far the greater part of the

---

[1] These descriptions are very common on tomb-stones, *e.g.* Wilmanns 2482, 2483, 2485.

[2] 'Prose-writers were also used for the purpose, such as Cicero, as is plain from the commentaries of Asconius,' says Becker, *Gallus*, ii. 82. 'That prose-writers, and in particular Cicero, as Bernhardy, *Roem. Lit.* p. 62, assumes, were also explained I can not find anywhere proved,' says Marquardt, *Privatl.* p. 106, note 7. Cicero writes to his brother (*ad Quint.* iii. 1, 4), 'meam orationem in illum (Calventium Marium) pueri

time of the pupils was given to poetry. 'Ars grammatica praecipue consistit in intellectu poetarum,' says a Latin grammarian (Serg. iv. p. 486, ed. Keil). Cp. Cicero, *Tusc. Disp.* ii. 11, 27: 'haec (sc. the works of the poets) nos, docti scilicet a Graecia, et a pueritia legimus et discimus : haec eruditionem liberalem et doctrinam putamus.'

The rule at Rome as in Greece was always to begin with

Homer.   Homer[1]. Quintilian remarks (i. 8, 5) that this is an excellent practice, not that his merits will be appreciated while the judgment is still but weak, but there is time for this afterwards, and he will not be read once only. Meanwhile the elevation of the poetry and the greatness of the theme will have an inspiring effect. The same was true of Vergil, who was introduced into the school course by Q. Caecilius Epirota, a freedman of Atticus, not long after the poet's death, and always held a place of preeminence. Other recent poets were also lectured upon by the same critic (Sueton. *Gramm.* 16). The influence which cliques of teachers might have in promoting or retarding the popularity of a poet is indicated by Horace (*Ep.* i. 19, 40), 'non ego...grammaticas ambire tribus et pulpita dignor.' In Greece it was nothing uncommon for both the Iliad and the Odyssey to be known by heart (Xen. *Symp.* **3,** 5). At Rome something less was

---

omnes tamquam dictata perdiscant,' but this may refer to those who were at the next stage, studying rhetoric rather than literature. On the other hand there is evidence to bear out Cicero's phrase (*de Orat.* i. 42, 187), 'in grammaticis poetarum pertractatio, historiarum cognitio, verborum interpretatio, pronuntiandi quidam sonus.' History was regarded, according to Quintilian's own definition (x. 1, 31), as 'proxima poetis et quodam modo carmen solutum,' written 'ad narrandum non ad probandum' and therefore coming within the sphere of pure literature. Cicero contrasts it with forensic oratory in *Orat.* 20, 66.

[1] Cp. Plin. *Ep.* ii. 14: 'sic in foro pueros a centumviralibus causis auspicari, ut ab Homero in scholis.' Horace in describing his school days (*Ep.* ii. 2, 42) says : 'Romae nutriri mihi contigit atque doceri, iratus Graiis quantum nocuisset Achilles.'

usually attempted, but the poems were known with extra-ordinary thoroughness. A teacher was expected to be able to answer all the countless questions which arose out of the text[1]. Homer would furnish abundant material, not only for the study of the language, but also for the elucidation of points of ancient history and mythology, geography and religion, manners and customs.

Quintilian has a high idea of the varied knowledge required of the *grammaticus*. He says (i. 4, 4), 'nor is it enough to have read the poets : every kind of writer must be studied, not only on account of the histories contained in them, but also for the language; for words often derive their rights from the authorities which sanction them. Further *grammatice* cannot be complete without music, as we have to treat of metres and rhythms : and if a man is ignorant of the stars, he cannot understand the poets, who, to pass over other points, so often use the risings and settings of constellations as indications of time. Nor can the professor of literature be ignorant of philosophy, not only because of many passages in almost all poems derived from a close and exact knowledge of the problems of nature, but also because of the poems of Empe-docles in Greek and Varro and Lucretius in Latin, writers who have taught in verse the doctrines of philosophy.' He goes on to argue that no little eloquence is also needed to speak with appropriateness and copiousness on such topics, and that a branch of study is by no means to be despised, which affords the indispensable basis for the higher training of the future orator.

---

[1] The puzzles in Juvenal (vii. 231–236) are all from Vergil : the name of the nurse of Anchises, the native land of Anchemolus, the age of Acestes and the number of jars of wine that he gave to the Trojans : and Prof. Mayor justly remarks that Servius would have furnished many more. Suetonius (*Tib.* 70) says of Tiberius : 'grammaticos eiusmodi fere quaestioni-bus experiebatur : "quae mater Hecubae?" "quod Achilli nomen inter virgines fuisset?" "quid Sirenes cantare sint solitae?"'

But while Homer was the invariable basis of literary study, the pupils were by no means confined to him.

Other Authors studied. Boys, not yet of an age for the more thorough training in style given in the schools of the rhetoricians, were taught to tell the fables of Aesop in pure and simple language (Quint. i. 9, 2). Hesiod with his prudential morality, his homely common sense, and his practical maxims, was a favourite school book; Cicero (*Ep.* vi. 18, 5) would have the son of his friend Lepta learn his Hesiod by heart, though he is as yet too young to appreciate Cicero's own *Orator*. Quintilian (i. 8, 6) approves of the tragedians; the lyric poets he thinks should only be read in selections; amatory elegies and hendecasyllables (which would generally be of a satiric character) should be banished altogether or reserved for a riper age. Comedy is especially useful for the future orator, but it must be studied with the same reservation as to the age of the pupil. Menander seems to have been always a favourite, doubtless owing to his happy sententiousness. Statius (*Silv.* ii. 1, 114) couples him with Homer as the subjects of a boy's studies: 'seu gratus amictu Attica facundi decurreret orsa Menandri.' The two go together as late as Ausonius (*Protr. ad Nep.* 46): 'conditor Iliados et amabilis orsa Menandri evolvenda tibi.' Of the bishop Fulgentius we read that as soon as he had thoroughly mastered Homer, his mother would have him read much of Menander. Statius (*Silv.* v. 3, 146–175) gives a long list of the Greek poets who were studied and paraphrased in his father's school at Naples, but we must remember that this was in a city which was largely or mainly Greek, and in the most distinguished school of its time. Ovid (*Trist.* ii. 70) speaks of Menander as read by boys and girls, although none of his plays is without some love-affair. We find less reference than we should have expected to the tragedians, but the protest of Augustine (*de Civ. Dei*, ii. 8) against the place given to stage-plays in education shows that they were so used in his time, and we cannot doubt that Quintilian is only sanctioning the usual practice in approving of their study. The Greek poets of Alexandria do not appear to have been studied in the Roman schools. Popular as they were under the early Empire, the tradition of the Greek teachers seems to have kept them out of the ordinary curriculum, and their influence, which was great, was mostly indirect through poets such as Catullus, Propertius and Ovid.

In the schools of Latin literature the place of Vergil, at all events after his death, was comparable to that of Homer in the Greek schools. It is rather curious that we find no mention of any translation of the Iliad before the time of Sulla; but the old translation of the Odyssey by Naevius was one of the chief text-books in the boyhood of Horace. A place of hardly less honour was given to the *Annals* of Ennius. The dramatists like Pacuvius, Accius, Afranius, Plautus, Caecilius, and Terence were also studied; but under the early Empire there seems to have been a reaction against the older writers. Along with Vergil, though not without excisions, Horace made his way into the schools, and we read that the poems of Lucan, of Statius, and even of Nero were lectured upon during the lifetime of their authors. But when Ovid boasts of the glory which he had won while still living, he is certainly thinking more of the general reading public than of boys in schools, as some have supposed. In any case the choice of authors seems to have been left entirely to the teacher, subject to the general principle 'non multa sed multum.' Whatever was studied, was studied with minuteness and with great diligence and known thoroughly.

Quintilian (i. 4) divides grammar into two parts: 'recte loquendi scientia' and 'poetarum enarratio.' He points out that both divisions of the subject involve a good deal more than might at first appear. It is not a matter of any great difficulty to distinguish consonants from vowels, or semi-vowels from mutes. But a precise exactness is required of those who would make a closer study of what we should now call phonetics. For instance, are any letters wanting in the Latin

Grammar.

alphabet? How are we to express the middle vowel in the word which is not exactly '*optumus*' nor yet '*optimus*'? Or are any redundant, such as *k* and *q*? Are any of the vowels ever used as consonants, as when *uos* (*vos*) is written in the same way as *tuos*? What is to be done when two or even three vowels come together? A pupil must learn what there is distinctive in letters and what common element, so that *e.g.* he may not be surprised to find that the diminutive of *scamnum* is *scabillum*. He must be familiar with the changes which are brought about by inflexion, as *cado, cecidi*, or by composition, as *calcat, exculcat*; and not less with those which have come about in the history of the language; e.g. *Lares, clamor, mersare, hordeum, bellum* were the forms current in his own time, for which in older days men said *Lases, clamos, mertare, fordeum, duellum*. (In this section Quintilian gives us much which is of the greatest value for the history of the Latin language.) Then the pupil must go on to study the parts of speech. The number of these has been disputed. The ancients, including Aristotle, recognised only verbs, nouns and conjunctions. Philosophers, especially the Stoics, added others; to conjunctions they added articles and prepositions, to nouns the substantive (*appellatio*) and the pronoun, to the verb the participle and the adverb. The Latin language did not need the article, but it recognised the interjection. Other divisions of the parts of speech had been proposed, which Quintilian did not approve, and the system of the Roman grammarians has been until recently that universally adopted.

The next thing to be thoroughly mastered is the inflexion of nouns and verbs. Many teachers neglect this, wishing to make a display of their pupils' progress in more showy branches, but they get on all the more slowly for their short cut, and they never really master what should follow. Under this head however Quintilian includes more than we might have expected. A good teacher *e.g.* will not be satisfied with teaching about the three genders and words that are common to two or to more.

He will explain how a word feminine in form may sometimes denote a male, as '*Murena*,' or a neuter form a female, as '*Glycerium*.' He will also—and this seems to us to be straying rather wide of his theme—enquire into the origin of names, and especially of cognomina, where this is no longer obvious, as with *Sulla, Agrippa, Vopiscus, Cotta*, and many others. Then there are questions as to the nature and number of the cases; there is nothing 'ablative' for instance in such an instrumental construction as 'percussi hasta.' The ordinary inflexions of verbs may be assumed to be known: 'litterarii paene ista sunt ludi et trivialis scientiae.' Still some ambiguous forms may cause difficulty. Words like '*lectum*' and '*sapiens*' might be either participles or substantives: the deponent imperatives '*fraudator*' and '*nutritor*' look like nouns. Impersonal passives, and irregular inflexions, such as that of '*fero*,' call for explanation.

Next the diction will need to be studied, which should be (1) correct, (2) clear, and (3) elegant. To secure the first we must avoid *barbarism*, which is a faulty use of an individual word, and *solecism*, which consists in an incorrect combination of words. Barbarism is shown sometimes in the use of a foreign word, sometimes in the capricious or ignorant variation of a Latin word. Under this head too come false quantities and other errors in pronunciation and in accent, of which Quintilian gives many examples. If all these errors are avoided the result will be 'correct speech' (ὀρθοέπεια). Solecisms arise when one or more words are incorrect in their present combination: as *e.g.* when to the question 'quem video?' the answer is given 'ego.' Hence it can be found 'in uno verbo' but not 'in solo verbo.' The author goes on to illustrate the nature of solecisms with some fulness, but not systematically, for, as he says, he is not writing a grammatical treatise. The mention of imported words leads him into a digression on the correct way of declining words borrowed from the Greek, which is followed by another on the limits of composition

in Latin words, which are much narrower than those allowed
in Greek, and by a warning against the danger of coining
words.   Then he goes on to consider what authorises diction,
and finds four bases on which it can rest:—*ratio, vetustas,
auctoritas,* and *consuetudo.*   The first, which we may perhaps
render 'theory,' relies mainly on analogy, whereby what is uncertain is established by something similar which is certain.
But it is sometimes aided by etymology.   There is a certain
dignity and almost sanctity attaching to what is archaic.
Orators and historians will furnish authority; poets are less safe
guides, because of the constraints of metre.   But the *certissima
loquendi magistra* is usage, and the diction employed must be
current coin.   He proceeds to give many interesting instances
of the application of analogy, and others in which it fails us, 'for
when men were first made, analogy was not sent down from
heaven to give them a fashion of speech, but was discovered
when they were already talking, and it was noticed in language
how each word came out....Analogy itself was created by nothing
but usage.'   On etymology he has some cautions to give,
which the progress of the science of language would lead us to
emphasise, and some of the examples which he gives of proposed etymologies sound to us like very bad jokes; but he is
himself quite conscious of their absurdity.   Care must be taken
that archaic words when employed are not so obsolete as to be
unintelligible; and in the same way no authority can justify
the use of words which the hearer cannot understand.   As for
usage we must remember that this means the usage of scholars,
not of the mob.   With regard to orthography 'recte scribendi
scientia' he points out that the elementary rules are not a
matter for the *grammaticus*; they will have been learnt in the
primary school; and disputed questions, of which he gives some
examples by no means without interest, are best left to the
judgment of the teacher.   His own opinion is that the closer
spelling can follow the pronunciation the better.   The treatment of elegance of diction he leaves to the rhetoricians.

Such are the general outlines of the grammar which the greatest schoolmaster of his day would have taught in the schools. Some, he tells us, thought many of these questions too petty to trouble pupils with, but he argues that such training is not harmful to those who pass through it, but only to those who linger too long over it ; and he confirms his own judgment by that of high authorities, including Cicero, who 'artis huius diligentissimus fuit et in filio recte loquendi asper quoque exactor.'

As for text-books we do not know of any in the time of the **Text-books** Republic, either prepared or adapted for use in **of Grammar.** schools. Treatises on questions of grammar had been written at an early date by men like L. Aelius Stilo Praeconinus, the first who wrote with competent learning and a philosophic breadth of view ; and the poet Lucilius gave much space to the discussion of points of orthography and grammar. But writers such as these appealed to scholars, not to learners. The teacher had to take some Greek compendium as his guide, and adapt it as best he might to the requirements of his Roman pupils, a task which was of course made all the easier by the fact that his teaching was naturally expected to be oral. The Greek book generally selected for this purpose was the elementary treatise of Dionysius Thrax (born about 166 B.C.). His little manual of barely 16 pages 'remained the standard work on grammar for at least 13 centuries' (Sandys, *Hist. of Class. Scholarship*, i. p. 137). The first Latin grammar intended expressly for use in schools was compiled by the teacher of Quintilian, the famous Q. Remmius Palaemon. It must have been written early in the reign of Vespasian. We probably have the substance of it in Quintilian's own treatise. From this time onwards Latin grammars were produced in great abundance, so that collections of such as are extant are very voluminous. The remark has been justly made that there seems to have been something in the study of grammar especially congenial to the somewhat rigid and prosaic turn of the Roman temper. But the writers upon it kept to the same general lines and differed only on unimportant details.

The second part of the teacher's duty—the 'poetarum enarratio'—Quintilian introduces with some re-marks on reading. This can only be taught in actual practice; it is not possible to give any general rules for raising or lowering the voice, for pronouncing more rapidly or more slowly, and the like. The main thing is a proper understanding of the passage to be read. Great care must be taken that the reading of poetry does not fall into an affected modulation of the voice. The difference between verse and prose must be marked but not exaggerated. Quintilian quotes a remark of Caesar when a boy, addressed apparently to a fellow-pupil: 'if you are singing, you are singing badly; if you are reading, you are singing.' Nor should the personifica-tion of characters be carried so far as on the stage. A reader is not required to act his parts. 'Lectio' was the first of the four stages which Varro laid down for the study of literature; Atticus had a high reputation for his skill as a reader, and Quintilian was proud of his son's promise in this respect (vi. Prooem. 11). An inscription at Rome (*C. I. L.* vi. 9447) runs: 'I have been a grammarian and a reader, but one of those readers who please by the purity of their diction.'

The Inter-pretation of Poetry.

For the proper reading of verse of course some knowledge of metre was required. The earliest national poems had been written in the rude Italian verse known as Saturnian, the exact nature of which is still a matter of discussion among scholars. It seems certain however that like most modern verse it was based upon accent. The Greek metres were regulated by quantity, *i.e.* by a definite sequence of long and short syllables, and the writers who had brought the Greek poetry to the knowledge of the Romans had as a rule adopted Greek measures for their translations, not however without certain licenses and variations; and these—both rules and exceptions—had to be made the matter of the most exact

Metre.

study. Special treatises on metre were composed by Ennius—according to Suetonius not the famous poet but a later writer of the same name[1]—Epicadus, a freedman of Sulla, Varro, who left nothing untouched, and Caesellius Vindex, a contemporary of Augustus. Even boys, says Quintilian, understand the nature of metrical feet, from which it is plain that it was one of the earliest subjects taught in schools. As soon as this was mastered, the teacher would explain to his pupils how to recognise them in a piece of verse. There is extant a fragmentary commentary by Priscian on the first twelve lines of the Aeneid, which probably is a fair specimen of the kind of teaching usual in the schools. It begins with a discussion of the verse, which includes a pretty full treatment of the laws of the hexameter metre. The teacher in reciting the lines would mark off the divisions of the feet either by snapping his fingers ('crepitu digitorum,' Quint. ix. 4, 55), by a stroke of his thumb (Hor. *Carm.* iv. 6, 35), or perhaps more frequently by stamping with the foot. In view of the fact that Epic poets were generally the earliest to be studied, pupils would commonly begin with the hexameter; and the Latin grammarians have much to say in praise of its varied beauties and capabilities, which were studied in the greatest detail. Next to this would come the trimeter iambic, the metre most extensively used in dramatic literature, comedy and tragedy alike. It is very curious to note that the licenses allowed in comic verse seem to have been less clearly understood by Horace and even by Cicero than they are by scholars of our own day[2]. Questions of rhythm held a hardly less important place in prose than in

[1] Cp. Teuffel, *Rom. Lit.* § 159, 13.

[2] Horace (*A. P.* 270 ff.) implies that neither the rhythm nor the wit of Plautus would have found favour, if his contemporaries had had as good taste as the men of Horace's own day. Cicero says expressly (*Orat.* 55, 184), 'comicorum senarii propter similitudinem sermonis sic saepe sunt abiecti ut nonnunquam vix in eis numerus et versus intellegi possit'—a confession which a modern scholar would be slow to make.

verse; but they seem to have been reserved for the higher stage, *i.e.* for the teaching of the rhetoricians.

The *lectio* of the pupils was, as we have seen, preceded by the *praelectio* of the teacher. The latter would first read or recite the passage himself, then each pupil would read it and be corrected, unless indeed the class was a large one, when only one would read, and the rest would listen to the criticisms addressed to him[1].

Explanation of the Text.

Next to the *lectio*, in Varro's division, came the *enarratio* or explanation of the text. This naturally made the greatest calls upon, and gave the best chances for the display of the erudition of the teacher. A *grammaticus* of repute was supposed to have at his fingers' ends all the knowledge needed to explain the incidents and allusions in the books usually studied, and to be able to illustrate them by appropriate stories. The popular collection 'Factorum et Dictorum Memorabilium Libri Novem' by Valerius Maximus, so largely read in the Middle Ages, has been not unreasonably supposed to have been drawn up for the use of teachers. We have noticed already (p. 58 note) the trivial and absurd pedantry into which this *enarratio* was apt to fall, and we cannot wonder that Seneca brands it with the contemptuous name of 'litterarum inutilium studia'; but if kept within due bounds the method must have quickened and satisfied an intelligent curiosity better than any other possible at that time. Some of the great teachers of the Renascence show us clearly what fruitful results in the most diverse fields can be gained by the minute study of classic poets. The various definitions of this branch of a teacher's duty prove how wide was the range which it covered; one generally accepted was 'obscurorum sensuum quaestionumque narratio' (Keil, *Gramm. Lat.* vii. p. 376); another less comprehensive 'secundum poetae voluntatem uniuscuiusque descriptionis explanatio' (*ib.* vi. p. 188). Of course the life of the poet, and the circumstances

[1] Quintil. ii. 5, 4–6.

under which the poem was composed would fall to be discussed. In the case of dramas there would be the date and conditions of their first representation, on which such information was given as has often been preserved to us in the *didascaliae* of the Greek, and the *indices* of the Latin plays. Mythology naturally entered largely into the matter of both epics and dramas, and the Christian Fathers complain bitterly of the time spent in school on the legends of Paganism. Cicero (*in Verr. Act.* ii. 1, 18, 47) assumes that Verres, if he had had a decent school education, would have naturally been familiar with the story of Latona and her children. We may notice that Quintilian gives much less space to the *enarratio historiarum* than he does to the *ratio loquendi.* This is partly because he seems to assign to the former a much narrower range than some other authorities had done. Partly it is due to the sensible view which he takes of the duties of a teacher: 'mihi inter virtutes grammatici habebitur aliqua nescire.' He tells us of a certain Didymus, who had written more than any one, and who criticised a story as quite absurd until it was shown to him in one of his own books. It is a great waste of time to try to understand everything which even the most worthless author has written: 'nam receptas aut certe claris auctoribus memoratas exposuisse satis est.' But here he seems to be limiting his remarks to one division of the *enarratio*, to which a much wider extension was often given. Perhaps his words refer not so much to the elucidation of narratives, occurring in the work under study, as to the illustration of sentiments or maxims found in them by means of appropriate anecdotes. In any case the limits of the explanation given to the text of an author were only fixed by the knowledge or the good sense of the teacher.

The next duty of the *grammaticus*, according to Varro, lay **Correction of Text.** in the *emendatio*. Of this there were two kinds which in practice ran into one another more than would seem natural to us. The first dealt with the correctness of the text in the hands of the pupils. This question was a very different one at Rome from what it had been in Greece. The scholars of Alexandria had to establish a sound text, especially in the case of Homer, by a careful collation of copies containing varying traditions, and by the most exact study of the poet's usage and the requirements of the context. At Rome the task was much less difficult. From the first, care seems to have been taken that there should be authoritative texts of the leading poets; thus Suetonius (*de Gramm.* 2) tells us that C. Octavius Lampadio edited with a commentary the *Punic War* of Naevius, and Q. Vargunteius did the same service for the *Annals* of Ennius, after they had already been edited by Lampadio (cp. Suet. u.s. Gell. xviii. 5, 11), in the generation after the death of the last-named critic[1]. The differing readings of later copies were due as a rule to the carelessness or ignorance of copyists. It was therefore a great point to secure MSS. as old as possible and derived from the best sources. Aulus Gellius delights to quote the evidence of copies 'mirandae vetustatis': cp. *e.g.* ii. 3, 5; v. 4, 1 etc.: and Cicero (*Orat.* 48, 160) quotes 'ipsius antiqui libri' to decide how Ennius spelt a word. Of course if it was possible to consult the author's own autograph, this carried the greatest weight; and Quintilian professes to have done this in the case of Cicero and Vergil ('quo modo et ipsum et Vergilium quoque scripsisse manus eorum docent'), and also Augustus ('in epistulis quas sua manu scripsit aut emendavit': i. 7, 20). Gellius too (xiii. 9, 14, 7) quotes an assertion of some critics that they had consulted the 'ideograph' of Vergil. Elsewhere (xviii. 5, 11) he tells us of the trouble and expense to which a scholar had been put to hire a MS. of Ennius which was said to have been corrected by the hand of Lampadio, that he might ascertain if in a certain line the poet had written 'equus' or 'eques.' This was rather a mechanical kind of business, depending on authority rather than learning or good judgment: and we do not find that textual criticism was in very

[1] Cp. Teuffel, *Rom. Lit.* § 138.

high esteem, though disputed points were contested with no little energy and even acerbity. Gellius (ii. 14, 3) calls those scholars 'nequam et nihili' who do not recognise that *stitisses* and not *stetisses* is the right reading in a passage of Cato, and in another place (xii. 10, 3) crushes by the weight of authority certain 'agrestes et indomitos certatores.' Sometimes the opinion of an expert was taken on the correctness of a MS. offered for sale. Gellius (v. 4, 1) tells us how he was sitting once in a bookseller's shop when a discussion arose over a copy of the *Annals* of Fabius. The seller declared that it was faultless; a *grammaticus* 'ab emptore ad spectandos libros adhibitus' said that he had found an error. The question was whether *duo et vicesimo* was a legitimate form. Of course a uniform text was necessary for teaching purposes, and so a high standard, if not of absolute correctness at any rate of uniformity, was maintained in the traditional text. The need of care to secure this comes out plainly from Cicero's words to his brother (*ad Quint.* iii. 5 and 6, 6): 'de Latinis vero, quo me vertam nescio; ita mendose et scribuntur et veneunt.' Hence one of the first duties of a teacher was to see that the texts in the hands of his pupils agreed with one another. Gellius (ii. 3, 5) tells us how a famous grammarian showed him a very ancient copy of the Second Book of the Aeneid, which was said to have belonged to Vergil himself, in which the spelling *aena* was corrected into *ahena*. It is obvious that the pupils' texts must have agreed on points such as this, if the teacher's comments were to be followed with intelligence.

Questions of what is now, rather unfortunately, called the Higher Criticism, dealing with the authorship and integrity of literary works, were left, as a rule, to the schools of rhetoric. But the second function of *emendatio* was the criticism of the author's style. Here the grammarians were accustomed to proceed with great freedom and boldness, even the most famous writers not escaping their censures. They acted fully up to the rule of Quintilian (x. 1, 24), 'neque id statim

Criticism of Style.

legenti persuasum sit, omnia quae optimi auctores dixerint utique esse perfecta...summi enim sunt, homines tamen.' It was their duty (*ib.* i. 8, 14) 'to detect all that is barbarous, improper, or contrary to the laws of language.' Gellius gives us in more than one place (cp. especially ii. 6) criticisms which had been passed on the language of Vergil. *Vexasse* was thought to be too weak a word to be applied (*Ecl.* vi. 76) to the damage done by Scylla to ships; and *illaudati* far too gentle an epithet for the tyrant Busiris (*Georg.* iii. 5). It is a faulty expression to say 'squalentem auro' (*Aen.* x. 314), for the ugliness connoted by *squalor* is inconsistent with the glitter and brightness of gold. To these and other similar criticisms Gellius gives what we may be sure were the answers current by tradition in the schools, and if sometimes the criticism seems to us somewhat shallow or the defence a little sophistical, they show at least the care with which the text of the poet was studied. Naturally it was not only the diction which was criticised. Gellius (ix. 10, 6) tells us how a distinguished grammarian, Annaeus Cornutus, the teacher of the poet Persius, to whom were due the criticisms quoted above, found fault with Vergil for not managing skilfully a figurative expression which he employs (*Aen.* viii. 406). The moderate and seasonable use of metaphors was felt to add brilliance to style; but if they are too numerous or far-fetched they only produce obscurity and disgust (Quint. viii. 6, 14). The effect of the order of words had to be explained and illustrated by the teacher (*ib.* ix. 4, 23). Care had to be taken that the arrangement of words in a sentence did not bring together either vowels or consonants which sounded harshly in juxtaposition. And in particular the teacher is to impress upon his pupils any merits or defects which there may be in the structure of the work as a whole, in the selection of topics and reflexions, and in knowing where a fuller treatment is in place, and where conciseness is required.

It was evidently impossible to draw a hard and fast line between such treatment of literary works and that which was appropriate to the school of rhetoric; hence there were many complaints that the *grammaticus* encroached on the sphere of the rhetorician. (Cp. p. 77.)

So far as to the duties of the teachers. But what meanwhile **Exercises of** were the tasks of the pupils? Can we learn the **the Pupils.** kind of exercises which were set to them at the various stages of their study of literature? Happily Quintilian gives us full and interesting information on this point (i. 9, 1 sqq.).

The first step was for the pupil to reproduce, either by word of mouth or in writing, the substance of a story told by the teacher. Fables, especially those of Aesop, were commonly employed for this purpose, as furnishing simple and brief narratives. Here clearness and correctness of style were the chief things aimed at. Then the pupil had to make his first attempt at paraphrase. At first he was not required to do much more than to turn verse into prose; then he was expected to give the sense in other words, and finally to paraphrase more boldly, abbreviating or embellishing, yet so as to preserve the sense. But paraphrase, as Cicero observed[1], is open to the objection that a great writer will have already expressed his meaning in the best way possible, so that it is apt to amount only to practice in putting worse words in the place of better ones. Hence it has been well urged of late that only second-rate pieces of literature should be set for paraphrase. Quintilian (x. 5, 5) does not altogether agree with this[2]. Then followed the treatment of themes (*sententiae*), or reflexions, which, if put into the mouths of definite persons, were called *chriae*[3]. Great store was set, both in speaking and writing, on a command of an abundance of general truths or commonplaces[4]; and even

[1] *de Orat.* i. 154.

[2] 'Ab illis dissentio, qui vertere orationes Latinas vetant, quia optimis occupatis, quidquid aliter dixerimus, necesse sit esse deterius.'

[3] These also may be treated *apud grammaticos*, because the necessary material is supplied by literature.

[4] Buecheler, *Carm. Lat. Epig.* i. 434, quotes the inscription on the tomb of a boy who died at the age of ten years and some months, in which we read 'dogmata Pythagorae sensi studiumque sophorum et libros legi.'

at school boys were trained to commit them to memory, to expand them and to illustrate them from history. The first stage of the expansion was of a very mechanical character, involving merely a change in the form of the *sententia* by the use of different cases; but obviously there was an opportunity for the employment of any amount of ingenuity and rhetorical skill[1]. Finally the pupils wrote little stories from the material supplied by the poets; but we are rather surprised to learn from Quintilian (i. 9, 6) that this was more to make them familiar with the matter than to improve their style, 'notitiae causa, non eloquentiae tractandas puto.'

Translation was, as we have seen, invented by the Romans as a means of literary training; there was nothing of the kind in Greece. Yet it does not appear to have been much in use in ordinary schools. Quintilian does not mention it as part of the work of the *grammaticus*, nor even of the teacher of rhetoric in the first stage of his instruction. It was practised by those who had attained some proficiency in rhetoric, and by many who had passed out of the training school altogether, as the best means of improving their style, *e.g.* by Cicero in mature manhood. But from the point of view of style it seems to have been little used in schools. Possibly it may have been felt that the task of producing really artistic translation was too difficult for pupils, so long as the Latin language was so little plastic as it was when literary training was introduced into Roman schools, and that afterwards the conservatism natural to teachers hindered its more common adoption. It was only gradually that it became a part of the course[2].

[1] M. Jullien happily compares the way in which M. Jourdain in Molière (*Bourg. Gentil.* ii. sc. 6) turns about the line

'Belle marquise, vos beaux yeux me font mourir d'amour.'

The most instructive modern example of instruction in formal rhetoric is the *De Copia* of Erasmus (1511), which is an extraordinary storehouse of methods of variation, expansion, enrichment etc., as applied to Latin prose-writing.

[2] Prof. Henry Sidgwick says (*Miscellaneous Essays*, p. 297), ' Teaching the art of Rhetoric by means of translation only, is like teaching a man to climb trees in order that he may be an elegant dancer.'

It is somewhat curious that we have no definite information as to the place which was held among the exercises of the schools Verse-
writing. by composition in verse. This is probably due to the fact that the most systematic and complete account of Roman education which we possess, that of Quintilian, treats of it in its relation to the training of an orator, so that the practice of verse-writing might naturally pass unnoticed. But we have many references to the early age at which verses were produced, which presume a school training in the mechanism of rhythm and diction, and indeed this is almost implied in the studies of metrical questions, to which we have already referred. The *Phaenomena* of Aratus were rendered into verse—much of which is still extant—by Cicero 'admodum adulescentulo,' and Quintilian says (x. 5, 16), 'ideo mihi videtur M. Tullius tantum intulisse lumen eloquentiae, quod in hos quoque studiorum secessus excurrit.' Vergil had written his *Culex* by the age of sixteen; Persius had produced a play and other poetical works before he had laid aside the dress of boyhood; Ovid had only cut his beard—as he tells us in *Trist.* iv. 10, 57—once or twice when he recited poems in public; Lucan had written a poem at fourteen or fifteen. These and other instances which might be added, are quoted as cases of precocity; but they point to a widely diffused facility. Indeed there are phrases used of some of the Emperors which indicate this pretty plainly : *e.g.* of Nero, Tacitus (xiii. 3) says, 'Puerilibus annis...aliquando carminibus pangendis inesse sibi elementa doctrinae ostendebat,' while of Verus we read (Jul. Cap. *Ver.* 2), 'amavit in pueritia versus facere, post orationes.' This points to the fact, which is probable enough in itself, that verse-writing was practised with the *grammaticus*, and declamation with the *rhetor*. But the subjects will have been much the same. An interesting monument was discovered not long ago, erected by his mourning parents in honour of Q. Sulpicius Maximus. This boy, who died before he was twelve years of age, had gained the prize for Greek verse in A.D. 94 at the Capitoline Games, instituted by Domitian. He had composed ex tempore 43 hexameters describing how Zeus rebuked Helios for entrusting his car to Phaethon, a common theme for declamation: and these verses the parents had engraved upon his tomb for fear that posterity should think their opinion of his skill misled by their affection. (See Baedeker, *Guide to Rome*, 'New Capitoline Collection,' Room III.) The prize does not appear to have been limited to boys, like that for the *ephebi* at Athens, but Sulpicius must have been well trained to make success, where there were 52 competitors, possible. There is nothing surprising in the fact that the composition was in Greek; the younger Pliny wrote a tragedy in Greek at the age of fourteen. It is true that he adds humorously: 'I do not know what kind of one it was; it was called a tragedy[1].' But the purpose of these exercises, and such as Cicero wrote at school (Plutarch, *Cic.* 2), was simply to acquire a ready command of language; and those were wisest who, like Marcus Aurelius, wrote verses daily, showed them to no one, and burnt them each night.

It may be noted that, in spite of this graduated system of
Teaching mostly given by Lectures. exercises, the attitude of the pupils, at all events in the schools of literature, was much more passive than we should consider in accordance with sound method. Quintilian (ii. 5, 15) says, it is true, 'in omnibus fere minus valent praecepta quam experimenta.' But as a rule the *grammaticus* in explaining authors delivered eloquent pre-lections, and his hearers took down in their note-books as much as they could of his explanations and criticisms. The notes of lectures seem to have much resembled those of students nowadays: sometimes remarkably full and accurate, sometimes confused and teeming with blunders (Quint. ii. 11, 7). It is a probable conjecture that a string of carefully chosen epithets for great writers of the past, such as that given by

---

[1] Plin. *Ep.* vii. 4, 2: 'Nunquam a poetice...alienus fui; quin etiam quattuordecim annos natus Graecam tragoediam scripsi. Qualem? inquis. Nescio: tragoedia vocabatur.'

Horace[1], may have been derived from the traditional teaching of the school-room. Sometimes the notes of pupils found their way into circulation against the wishes of the teacher (Quint. *Prooem.* 7), as has also been the case in modern times. Sometimes however a master of eminence would publish his own notes—' profitentium commentariolos,' as Quintilian calls them. Out of the almost unlimited field of knowledge which was tilled by the grammarians as a body, each would choose his own special corner, and so, when his notes were published, each came to add something to the stores of learning to which later criticism is indebted so largely. (Cp. Jullien, *Les Professeurs de littérature*, pp. 279 ff.)

---

[1] Cp. Hor. *Ep.* ii. 1, 50–62.

CHAPTER V.

HIGHER STUDIES—RHETORIC AND PHILOSOPHY.

IN early days the ordinary schoolmasters (*grammatici*)
Schools of   taught the elements of rhetoric. So Suetonius
Rhetoric.   tells us (*de Gramm.* 4); and indeed there could
be no very clear line of division drawn between the exercises
used for training in style and those used for teaching effective
speech. Hence some speakers took part in public life with no
other training than that of the schools, and won distinction as
advocates (Suet. *ib.* 7 and 10). In Quintilian's time it was
recognised as the right thing that rhetoric should be taught
only in the special advanced schools conducted by the
rhetoricians. But he expresses and concurs in the common
complaint that boys are sent on—always to the Latin teachers
of rhetoric, and generally to the Greek—later than they should
be. This is due, he says, to the fact that the teachers of
rhetoric—the Latin especially—have neglected their own duty,
while the teachers of literature have usurped that of others.
The former limit themselves to teaching declamation, and that
only on themes adapted to deliberative assemblies or the law-
courts, while the latter not only pounce upon what the others
pass over, but seize even on topics which make the greatest
claims upon the speaker. The result is that pupils who are
due at higher training are kept hanging about at school, and
are not thought fit to be sent to a professor of declamation

before they know how to declaim. This complaint seems only in part justified. It is in the nature of things that a schoolmaster should wish to retain a promising pupil and teach him all he can ; and equally natural that the more advanced teacher. should like to have his student sent to him as soon as he is fit. But a good deal of the work done in the school of rhetoric with a view to special training was not less suitable for the general culture, and in particular for the formation of style, which was the business of the school. It need be no matter of surprise then if we find the exercises in the one class of school largely the same as those in the other, though with some differences both in method and in extent.

The order in which the preliminary rhetorical exercises— **Preliminary** called *progymnasmata*—were taken was a traditional **Exercises.** one, derived from the Greek usage. The exercises themselves closely resemble those which we have already noticed. The first is practice in narrative, with regard to which Quintilian (ii. 4, 2) would now drop the fable and the story (*argumentum*), though others would retain these if treated with sufficient freedom, and would confine the matter to history. On this follows naturally the critical treatment of narratives—what the Greeks called *anaskeue* and *kataskeue*, i.e. an attack on or a defence of the truth of the story. Then come panegyrics and invectives, which give a wide scope for oratory. The *chria* in rhetoric—so called, we are told, because it was the most useful of all the exercises—was much more developed than in literature. It became an exhaustive discussion, according to the rules of the art, of a sentiment ascribed to some definite person. The usual treatment was somewhat as follows : first the author of the saying was eulogised ; then his words were paraphrased and developed, so as to bring out the meaning. Next the truth of the thought was established, both positively and negatively, in the latter case by pointing out what results would follow if it were not true. Then came a comparison, an example drawn from history, confirmatory quotations from standard authors, and finally a conclusion, which often took the form of an exhortation. The *sententia* was treated in a very similar manner, which indeed has been the model on which the art of literary composition has been taught ever since, both in medieval and in more modern schools. Examples have been preserved to us of model exercises written by the teachers for the guidance of their pupils[1]. But all these exercises and the other *progymnasmata* were intended—in whatever kind of school they were employed—only as introductory to the main exercises of rhetoric, *i.e.* declamations.

Even if a boy had had some training in the preliminary exercises before he came to the rhetorician, his more serious work at them would begin there. Quintilian (ii. 4 ff.), in speaking of the earliest teaching of the master of rhetoric, 'cuius aliquid simile apud grammaticos puer didicerit,' treats first of narration, in the form of history, 'tanto robustior quanto verior,' in composing which he would have the greatest attention paid to style, and desires the pupil 'ante discat recte dicere quam cito.' Then follows the 'opus destruendi confirmandique narrationes,' the destructive or defensive criticism of stories, such as that of the raven which perched on the helmet of Valerius Corvus. Then follows the more difficult task of panegyric and invective, which is of especial value, partly from the varied demands which it makes upon the mental powers, partly from its developement of the moral judgment, and partly from the way in which it stores the memory with examples to be used on occasion. 'Commonplaces,' *i.e.* general reflexions on vices, are of immediate service in legal cases ; and even more so are 'theses,' *i.e.* abstract questions involving a comparison, such as 'is country life to be preferred to life in a town ? ' There are other 'theses' of a deliberative kind, *e.g.* 'should a man marry ? ' These if

Exercises in the School of Rhetoric.

---

[1] Cp. Jullien, *op. cit.* p. 303.

connected with a name become *suasoriae*—a term of which we shall hear again[1]. He speaks with favour of an exercise used by his own teachers, in which pupils had to divine the reason for something, as *e.g.* why Cupid was represented as a winged boy armed with arrows and a torch. The advocacy or criticism of laws calls for the utmost efforts of the speaker, involving as it does frequently questions of the greatest difficulty and importance, as well as of the greatest variety. These are the chief preliminary exercises by which the ancients trained the capacity for speaking. The practice of pleading in imaginary cases, as if actually in a law-court, was introduced, he says, by Demetrius Phalereus at Athens (circ. B.C. 320).

Before Quintilian goes on to speak of declamation proper, the special function of the rhetorician, he stops to point out how much advantage may be gained from the critical study with a teacher, not now of the poets, but of history and especially of orators. The pupils

Literature in Relation to Rhetoric.

must be trained to observe merits and faults, both of matter and of style, for themselves : 'nam quid aliud agimus docendo eos, quam ne semper docendi sint?' This training in careful criticism will be of more value than any amount of theoretical instruction, and pupils will much prefer to have the mistakes of others pointed out rather than their own. The best writers must be chosen—Livy rather than Sallust, who requires a more developed intelligence, but above all Cicero, who 'et iucundus incipientibus quoque et apertus est, nec prodesse tantum, sed etiam amari potest.' Neither the rough and archaic style of Cato and the Gracchi, nor the affected and over-ornate diction of Quintilian's own time, is to be taken as a model. Then he discusses the extent to which the teacher should offer suggestions to the student for the treatment of the subject, or should let him take his own course and afterwards correct him, and

---

[1] A good example of the *suasoria* is given by Juvenal (i. 15), where he claims to have received an ordinary school education : 'et nos consilium dedimus Sullae, privatus ut altum dormiret.'

prefers that there should be more of the former[1]. He greatly
approves of the practice of learning by heart, but not, as was
too commonly the case, the pupil's own compositions ; they
should not be allowed to recite from memory their own
productions until they have attained some excellence, and as a
reward of their progress. Then follows an interesting discussion
how far a pupil's strong points are to be developed and how far
effort should be directed towards removing his weaknesses,
raising thus the standing educational problem what amount of
uncongenial work is to be imposed upon pupils of marked
special capacity. He comes to the sensible conclusion that
weaker intellects must not be pressed beyond their natural
powers, but where there is more promising material, it must
receive as complete culture as possible. After these somewhat
discursive remarks on the preparatory studies Quintilian pro-
nounces the pupil who is well trained and practised in these,
ready to attack the subjects furnished by the *suasoriae* and
forensic cases. He has still however something to say on
the method and value of declamation. It is of late introduction,
but it is the most useful of all exercises. Indeed some think
that it is alone sufficient to develope eloquence. It has been
undervalued because of the absurd themes, out of all relation
with real life, which have been chosen as its subjects. It ought
to keep in view the kind of occasions for which the speaker is
being trained. In forensic cases art must be carefully concealed;
but there are times when a display of oratorical skill is in place,
in order to give pleasure to the audience. Quintilian (ii. 11)
then goes on to demonstrate the value of a systematic study of

[1] The office of the master in supplying the necessary information to his
pupils on the subject of their declamations was called his *sermo* ; and
in what are (wrongly) called the 'Declamations of Quintilian' we have
some interesting specimens of the *sermo*. He states and explains the
subject, shows how it may be treated, indicates the dangers and advantages
of various lines of argument, and generally does, as we might incline to say,
too much of the thinking for them.

rhetoric, as against those who believed in nothing but natural powers and practice. He adds a satirical description of those speakers who look for a supply of matter and language to the inspiration of the moment: and disproves the contention that untrained speakers have more force, and therefore more power with an audience. The trained, he maintains, lose only their faults; 'doctis est et electio et modus,' while the untrained pour out everything. It is only after these preliminary remarks that Quintilian goes on to define rhetoric, and to indicate in what way he means to treat it in the ten remaining books of his famous work.

It does not come within the scope of the present book to Theory of **describe** in detail the system of rhetoric which, Rhetoric. originating in Sicily in the 5th century B.C. and developed at Athens and afterwards in Asia Minor, had now become traditional in the schools of rhetoric at Rome[1]. But a few points may be worth noting. There were commonly recognised to be three kinds of oratory—the *genus demonstra-*

---

[1] Renan once said (*Discours de Reception de M. de Lesseps*), 'You have a horror of rhetoric, and you are right; it is (with poetics) the only mistake of the Greeks. After having produced masterpieces, they thought they could give rules for producing them—a serious mistake. There is no art of speaking, any more than there is an art of writing. To speak well is to think aloud. Oratorical and literary success has never any cause but one, absolute sincerity.' But thinking is one thing, and speaking another; and the pleasure derived from finished and beautifully modulated speech is as legitimate as that derived from any other form of art. It is one to which the Greeks, and under their teaching the Romans, were susceptible to a degree which we can hardly realise. Cp. Cicero, *Orat.* 50-1, 168–173: Capes, *University Life at Athens*, p. 88. But in addition to the aesthetic pleasure, there was also the practical usefulness of the art. The leading Greek and Roman statesmen were conscious that they did speak more effectively for having been trained (p. 27). At the beginning of the Civil War Pompeius took up again his practice of declamation, in order to be able to reply the better to Caesar's advocate Curio (Suet. *Rhet.* 1), though as Boissier (*Tacite*, p. 202) remarks, it was thought afterwards that he might have done better to raise legions.

tivum, the *g. deliberativum*, and the *g. iudiciale*. In the first the speaker makes a display of his own powers, usually in the way of panegyric or invective; in the second he endeavours .to persuade his audience to take some action; in the third he tries to establish the guilt or innocence of some one who is arraigned before a court of law. In all these forms of oratory there are five tasks which devolve upon the speaker, for which he has to receive instruction: (1) *inventio*, the devising of appropriate matter; (2) *dispositio*, or arrangement; (3) *elocutio*, the clothing of the matter in proper language; (4) *memoria*, remembrance of the arguments, the order and the language; (5) *pronuntiatio*, the delivery, including not only the management of the voice, but also gestures. Quintilian allots three books (iv.–vi.) to *inventio*, one (vii.) to *dispositio*, two (viii.–ix.) to style, including tropes and figures of speech; in the tenth book he diverges into a review of Latin literature from the point of view of the orator; in the eleventh he deals with adaptation, with memory, and with delivery; in the twelfth he takes up various moral and intellectual requisites for success as an orator. His treatise preserves for us in the most interesting, though not the most systematic form the theory of rhetoric[1], which underlay the practical training especially in Greece; and as we observe the moderation and good sense, which mark his treatment throughout, we do not wonder that he ranked as the most eminent teacher of his day.

But whatever the value of a sound basis of theory, the main thing was practice in declamation. This was not solely a matter for the school. Cicero (*Brut.* 90, 310) says, 'com-
Declamation. mentabar declamitans (sic enim nunc loquuntur) saepe cum M. Pisone et cum Q. Pompeio aut cum aliquo cottidie; idque faciebam multum etiam Latine, sed Graece saepius.' He carried on this practice of declaiming in Greek

---

[1] The most systematic exposition of the theory is given in the anonymous treatise addressed 'ad Herennium,' and printed in Cicero's works. Cp. Cicero, *de Oratore* (Clarendon Press edition), Introd. pp. 51–64.

till the time of his praetorship, when he was forty years of age (Suet. *de Rhet.* 1). And even later on in his life he guided the practice of his younger friends Hirtius and Dolabella. This practice would doubtless be on the lines laid down in the schools, but in these there was, as Suetonius tells us, a certain variety of method, according to the tastes of the teachers. But in Cicero's time 'the understanding was strengthened and the range of knowledge extended by the writing out of essays on general topics, *proposita* as Cicero called them, as the Greeks called them θέσεις, and by the treatment of *communes loci*, or the topics which were sure to come up in the course of any serious discussion of a matter of practice. The written treatment of θέσεις and *communes loci* was the main if not the only exercise of originality known to the educationists of Cicero's day' (Nettleship, *Essays*, ii. p. 112). Cicero himself[1] divides *quaestiones* into the limited or concrete (*causae*) and the unlimited or abstract (*proposita*); but of these the latter were much preferred as subjects for declamation.

In the time of Quintilian declamations were commonly divided into *suasoriae* and *controversiae*. These names were not known to Cicero and his contemporaries[2]. (The word

---

[1] Cp. Cic. *Top.* 79: 'quaestionum duo genera, alterum definitum, alterum infinitum. Definitum est quod ὑπόθεσιν Graeci, nos causam : infinitum, quod illi θέσιν appellant, nos propositum possumus nominare. Causa certis personis, locis, temporibus, actionibus, negotiis cernitur aut in omnibus aut in plerisque eorum : propositum autem in aliquo eorum aut in pluribus nec tamen in maximis.' *Part. Orat.* 61 : 'Duo sunt quaestionum genera, quorum alterum finitum temporibus et personis causam appello, alterum infinitum nullis neque personis neque temporibus notatum propositum voco.' Cp. Prof. Mayor's notes on Quintilian x. in *Journal of Philology*, vol. xxix. p. 156, for many more reff.

[2] Cp. Boissier, *Tacite*, p. 205: 'Shortly afterwards the *theses* were replaced by *causae*, which indicated undoubtedly that the subjects which were treated in the school should resemble the cases which were pleaded before the judges ; then all of a sudden there is no further question of *theses* or of *causae*; we hear of *suasoriae* and *controversiae*, and the

controversia was used, but only in the sense of a dispute.) As the elder Seneca[1] said (*Praef. Controv.* 1), 'controversias nos dicimus, Cicero causas vocabat.' In both some supposed càse was taken in hand[2]—it might be from real life or purely imaginary—and then for the *suasoria* some course of action was discussed, for the *controversia* some proposition was maintained or denied. The former exercise was thought the easier, and the better adapted for beginners; it served as a training for deliberative oratory; while the latter was better suited to the more advanced and prepared for the oratory of the law-court, which was always regarded as making the severest demands upon speakers. We have a very interesting collection, dating from the time of Tiberius, and made by the elder Seneca, the father of the philosopher. It consists of seven *suasoriae* (one book), and five books (originally there were ten) of *controversiae*, together with some fragments, and instructive prefaces. These books contain, after the statement of the question, the points

scholastic exercise by which boys are trained to speak takes the name of *declamatio*, which in this sense is new.' Doubtless *causae* tended to drive out *theses*, but the former seem to have been in use from the first; and the latter were probably never wholly abandoned. Boissier goes on: 'If the need of a change of name was felt, it is probable that the thing also was changed; but no one tells us in what the change consisted, and it is impossible to know with certainty. We can only suspect that it must have had a certain importance, and that it was of a nature to satisfy the public, seeing that its success was so rapid and so complete.' The new form of exercises gave more room for ingenuity of rhetoric, and less for serious thought.

[1] Sometimes this writer is called Marcus Seneca, but there is no good authority for this; it is more likely that he was called Lucius, like his son the philosopher.

[2] There is a good example of the *causa*—which however he calls *controversia*—given by Suetonius (*de Rhet.* 1). Some slave-mongers, landing at Brundisium and wishing to avoid the import duty on a handsome and valuable young slave, dressed him in the garb of a free boy—the *bulla* and *toga praetexta* (p. 40). When they reached Rome the boy claimed his freedom, as having been emancipated by this act on the part of his owners.

which were made in arguing it on this side and on that by the most eminent rhetoricians of the time, conspicuous among whom is Porcius Latro, Seneca's own teacher. We cannot but be struck with the remarkable ingenuity shown both in devising problems of conflicting laws or moral claims, and in inventing conceivable solutions for them. Viewed as an intellectual gymnastic, this method of training was certainly not without its value. But there were serious drawbacks. In the first place the matter was much restricted in its range, and the subjects were few in number. To judge from the specimens preserved to us by Seneca, and those of a later date wrongly ascribed to Quintilian, the themes are strangely hackneyed, though there is great diversity in the treatment of them. Perhaps the declaimers liked to show their ingenuity in the treatment of familiar material—like the Greek tragedians—rather than in the invention of new. A still more serious fault was that the subjects were out of all relation with real life, and such as could not genuinely excite the interest or touch the feelings of the speaker. The most common source to draw from was the legends of the Greek mythology; and

What's Hecuba to him or he to Hecuba?

Even the laws, assumed to be binding, are often such as never existed anywhere. The consequence was that less and less attention was paid to the substance of the speech, and more and more to the language. Justness and appropriateness of thought came to be less esteemed than brilliance and novelty of expression[1]. It would take us too far out of our way to

[1] There is a vigorous attack on the evils resulting from the methods of 'the so-called rhetoricians' put into the mouth of Messalla, one of the characters in the Dialogue of Tacitus, *de Oratoribus*, cc. 30–35. He complains that by taking their pupils too young, and absorbing them prematurely in the tricks and quibbles of the rhetoric of the schools they leave no time for the broader studies of history and philosophy, and so have deprived their own art of the firm foundation on which it had been based in the days of Cicero. In all this he is probably expressing the views of

notice at length the injurious and almost fatal effects which this training in declamation had upon the literature of the Empire. But we may observe how much it was promoted by the common practice of public recitation. Not only were poets, from the days of Vergil and Horace onward, and professors of rhetoric accustomed to recite their productions before audiences of their friends and patrons[1], but boys at school were encouraged to make similar displays of their powers. When a pupil had elaborated a theme, not without help from the *sermo* of his teacher (cp. p. 81), he would learn it by heart, and declaim it in the presence of his father and his much enduring friends: 'nam ita demum studere liberos, si quam frequentissime declamaverint, credunt, cum profectus praecipue diligentia constet' (Quint. ii. 7, 1). Speeches produced in this way and for this purpose naturally aimed at making an immediate impression by glittering phrases and epigrammatic turns of thought. Besides, as the subjects were often such as had already been handled, sometimes over and over again, in verse, they naturally called up many poetic reminiscences of language as well as matter. Hence even the earliest declaimers, such as Arellius Fuscus, the master of Ovid, are full of imitations of Vergil: and poetical words, turns and manners of speech came to be dominant in prose. Of course the absence of all free political life contributed greatly to give an unreal character to rhetoric under the Empire. The power of speech, which to the statesmen of the Republic from Cato to Cicero had been—next

Tacitus himself. Unfortunately a gap in the MSS. makes his speech break off at a point where his discussion of the relation of rhetorical training to real life promises to be most interesting. In an earlier passage (c. 14) he had contrasted the practice of the *veteres oratores* and their broad culture with the narrow view of the *novi rhetores*.

[1] We are told that Asinius Pollio, the patron of Vergil, was the first to have invited his friends to a recital of his own compositions (Suet. *Ex. Contr.* iv.). All that is to be said about recitations is to be found in Professor Mayor's note on Juvenal iii. 9.

perhaps to success in war—the most potent aid to win office and power in political life, had now become merely a graceful accomplishment, serving to draw forth the plaudits of a dilettante audience. A method of training, which had justly found favour under the differing conditions of an earlier time, showed serious defects in later generations. But it is unfair to censure the education received by the Gracchi and Cicero, because, as a result of material changes, it had become ill adapted for the days of Nero or Domitian.

We must not indeed overlook the traces of a reaction against the training given by declamation which are to be found in the Latin literature itself. Quintilian's great work was entitled *Institutio Oratoria* and it describes in detail how a young man should be trained as a speaker ; but he takes his ideal for granted. He accepts the Ciceronian tradition, and teaches how it can be carried on under the conditions of his own day. But to others the ideal seemed different. Professor Nettleship (*Essays*, Second Series, p. 74) has shown how Eumolpus in Petronius may be regarded as a representative of another school. This felt the danger of declamation on unreal and hackneyed themes (cp. cc. 1 and 2), and the mistake of those who thought 'facilius poema extrui posse quam controversiam sententiolis vibrantibus pictam.' Poetry, and perhaps we may add the cultivated intelligence which can appreciate it, can only be produced when 'ingenti flumine litterarum inundata' (c. 118). (It is in this connexion that Petronius uses the famous phrase 'Horati curiosa felicitas.') So far as we can gather from scattered and sometimes obscure hints, there were not wanting those who protested against the tendency to make oratory the goal of literary education, and would have this education pursued for its own sake as intellectual culture.

It has been noticed already how the religious teaching of
Study of   the Roman boy was mainly a matter of learning the
Philosophy.   customary ritual observances, and being trained in
the traditional morals at home and at school. But something

more may here be said as to the teaching by which this was commonly supplemented as the pupil grew to manhood. For the upper classes at Rome, of whom alone we have adequate information, the guide of life was found far more in philosophy than in religion. To some extent under the Republic and still more under the Empire, the various Greek schools were coming to lay aside their speculative differences, and dwelling more on that moral teaching on which they agreed. From the first introduction of Greek philosophy at Rome it had been common for leading citizens to have professors of the subject resident in their houses. These have been called 'the domestic chaplains . of heathendom,' but the phrase is not an altogether happy one, as it suggests some duties in connexion with family worship. A better comparison is with the 'directors of conscience,' who often resided in noble Catholic families, to give their guidance and consolation as might be needed. Thus when Livia the wife of Augustus was in deep distress at the death of her younger son Drusus, Areus 'philosophus viri sui' consoled her more effectively than any one. Another philosopher who lived in the house of Augustus and was said to have had a great influence over him, was Athenodorus of Tarsus. Cicero took into his house Diodotus the Stoic, whose lectures he had heard as a youth, and he remained there till he died, four years after Cicero's consulship. To realise the training of a Roman boy of high family, we must keep in mind this daily informal education by association with those whose very profession required that they should be habitually familiar with great and elevating thoughts. Of course there were pretenders and hypocrites in this, as in every other age, and the trite superficiality of much of their talk gained for the name by which they were known—*aretalogi*, 'talkers on virtue'—a by no means respectful meaning. Sometimes, as in the case of Seneca, one philosopher might have a wide circle of younger friends to whom he acted as 'director,' and his letters to Lucilius show us how suggestive and penetrating this direction was. It is nominally based on Stoicism,

6—5

but his material is taken wherever he can find it, and he delights especially to clinch his arguments by a telling quotation from the leader of the antagonistic school, Epicurus.

But in addition to this informal and half-unconscious familiarity with the doctrines of philosophy, picked up in the home, we must not ignore the place given to its more systematic study. Here, as so often, it is hard to say how far cases are to be taken as typical. It would be a mistake for instance to suppose that every son of a quiet country gentleman of modest means had the education which was enjoyed by Cicero. His father, though not rich, was ambitious for him, and had access to the best circles of Roman society. If we read then that Cicero studied both rhetoric and philosophy in Greece, we must not at once assume that this was the usual practice. Yet examples enough are quoted to show that it must have been very common.

The study of philosophy was naturally begun as a rule at Rome. Thus Cicero before he put on the dress of manhood attended the lectures of Phaedrus the Epicurean at Rome; it is true that Phaedrus only happened to be at Rome owing to the unsettled state of things at Athens (B.C. 88). We learn without surprise that he made a complete convert of his young pupil. But when Cicero was eighteen years of age, Philo the head of the Academic school swept the teaching of Phaedrus out of his mind by the lectures which he delivered at Rome, and Cicero adopted those doctrines to which he remained faithful on the whole for the rest of his life. It was nearly ten years later, at the age of 27, that he went to Greece, mainly to recruit his health. Here he spent two years in studying both rhetoric and philosophy under the most eminent Greek professors at Athens, in Asia Minor, and especially at Rhodes. But the course which Cicero followed, owing to circumstances, at a comparatively late period of his life, was taken much earlier by others. Caesar indeed was 25 when he visited Rhodes to study

Higher Education in Greece.

rhetoric, but the younger Cicero and Ovid were only 20 when they went to what has been called with some latitude the 'University of Athens.' Horace appears to have begun his studies there at the age of 18, and we may perhaps regard 18–20 as the usual time for a Roman youth to visit Athens. Here he would find the recognised heads of the four great schools of philosophy, the Academic, the Peripatetic, the Stoic and the Epicurean, maintained partly by endowments bequeathed for the purpose, partly by the fees or presents of students who flocked thither from all parts of the civilised world. But the nucleus of the classes of at least the first three—the fourth was not so encouraged—was formed by the *Ephebi*. This name was given to the young Athenian citizens, just passing into manhood, for whom a special training was provided by the State. It was not all who could afford the necessary expenses; but those who could for the period of one year wore a common dress, went through the same military and athletic exercises, and attended the same religious services and the same courses of instruction. We have learnt much of recent years from extant inscriptions as to this brief collegiate course[1], so that we

---

[1] See W. W. Capes, *University Life in Ancient Athens* (1877). It is to be remembered that most of the information which we have relates to a period later not only than the days of Athenian liberty, but even than the period of Roman life which we have mainly in view. For instance, it was only from the fourth century B.C. onwards that there was any teaching of philosophy at Athens, and it was not systematised till a much later date.

It is not surprising to find that the philosophers and the rhetoricians were not always on the best of terms, and treated each the other's subject with some contempt. There was many an echo of the language of Vergil (*Catal.* v.):

> ite hinc, inanes, ite, rhetorum ampullae,
> inflata rhoso non Achaico verba:
> et vos...
> scholasticorum natio madens pingui,
> ite hinc, inane cymbalon iuventutis...
> nos ad beatos vela mittimus portus,
> magni petentes docta dicta Sironis,
> vitamque ab omni vindicabimus cura.

can understand better the surroundings of the young Romans who went to Athens for their higher education; but although after the loss of the political freedom of that city, the ranks of the Ephebi were by no means closed against foreigners, we find the names of very few Romans on the lists which have been preserved. Probably they preferred the greater freedom of 'unattached' students. For the Rector, called the *Kosmetes*, and the Proctors or *Sophronistae* administered a somewhat rigid, but if our authorities are to be trusted, a very successful control over their pupils. The total number of students seems to have been very large; Theophrastus alone, the successor of Aristotle, attracting more than 2000, and many of them were extremely poor; but like theology in the Middle Ages philosophy was to the student at once the keenest intellectual exercise and the only source of light on the problems of life and destiny, so that its attractive force was widely irresistible.

CHAPTER VI.

ENDOWMENT OF EDUCATION.

THE Empire of which Julius Caesar traced out the leading
Schools under lines was intended to blend Hellenic culture with
the Empire. the traditional principles of the Roman State. To
use the phrase of Mommsen, it was to be 'cosmopolitan.'
It does not therefore surprise us to find that the beginnings of
a system of State-schools were laid by Caesar, when he gave
the franchise[1] not only to all doctors who were living at Rome
or should settle there, but also to all teachers of liberal arts
(Suet. *Caes.* 42). Augustus in banishing foreigners from Rome
made an exception in favour of these (Suet. *Aug.* 42). But the
first endowment on the part of the State was due to Vespasian,
who 'was the first to endow Latin and Greek rhetoricians with a
stipend of 100,000 sesterces, to be paid from the Imperial
treasury[2]' (Suet. *Vesp.* 18). It is not however probable that
this annual salary of nearly £800 a year was paid to any

---

[1] It is putting the effect of this bestowal of the franchise rather strongly,
when Mommsen (iv. 567) says, 'Caesar initiated a revolution also in this
department.' He organised nothing in the way of a national system of
education, and there is very little evidence that he had such a system in
view. Vespasian, who did take some steps in that direction, was hardly a
prominent champion of the ideals of Caesar.

[2] 'Primus e fisco Latinis Graecisque rhetoribus annua centena constituit.'

rhetoricians but those of the capital. Some scholars have indeed held that it was universal, a meaning which the words of Suetonius would bear. But it is not likely· that such an extensive system, as this would imply, should have perished without leaving a trace, nor that all teachers, at home or in the country, should have been paid equally. Indeed it seems possible that this .endowment, though founded by Vespasian, was first actually paid by Domitian ; for Jerome under the year A.D. 92 says, ' Quintilianus ex Hispania primus Romae publicam scholam et salarium e fisco accepit et claruit.' At all events Quintilian is the first endowed professor who is known to us. Of later Emperors Hadrian was especially liberal in his patronage of professors of the liberal arts, with whom he liked to discuss. He built also an Athenaeum as a school for literature, where poems were recited and declamations delivered. But it is rather curious that we do not read of anything like University buildings at Rome, answering to the Museum for instance at Alexandria, where the professors of the various subjects could give their instruction under a common roof. Subsequent Emperors carried out the same policy in the provinces ; *e.g.* we read of Antoninus Pius (Jul. Capit. c. 11), ' rhetoribus et philosophis per omnes provincias et honores et salaria detulit.' Alexander Severus (Lamprid. c. 44), ' rhetoribus...salaria instituit et auditoria decrevit et discipulos cum annonis ('exhibitions') pauperum filios modo ingenuos dari iussit.' The costs were perhaps in some cases met from imperial funds, but as a rule they appear to have been charged on the municipalities. The interesting institution of the ' alimentarii pueri et puellae ' shows another step in the direction of the State regulation of education. It had long been customary for the poorer citizens to be aided by gratuitous distributions of corn, oil and money. Nero extended these grants from adults to children in need ; and Trajan provided that they should be made monthly both to orphans and to the children of poor parents. To all these children he undertook to give the *munus educationis* to the number of five thousand (Plin. *Paneg.* 26–28). We have records of the rules of administration on stones found at Veleia near Placentia, and also near Beneventum. Hadrian and both the Antonines extended the institution to the provinces ; but it seems always to have fallen far short of a systematic scheme of public education, which some have seen in it.

There is a very interesting letter of the younger Pliny (iv. 12) written to the historian Tacitus, and describing how he founded and endowed a school for the inhabitants of his own *municipium*, Comum. The young son of a fellow-burgher, when paying his respects at a morning call, said that he was a student at Milan. 'Why not at home ?' asked Pliny. 'Because we have no teachers here,' was the answer. Pliny pointed out to the fathers who were present that it would be an easy matter to combine and engage one ; this would save what they had now to spend on lodging and travelling. He himself, though childless, would contribute one-third of the necessary amount. He would have provided the whole, had he not feared that unless the parents had a direct interest in getting the best return for their money, corrupt influences might affect the choice, ' ut accidere multis in locis video, in quibus praeceptores publice conducuntur '—a phrase which shows that publicly endowed schools were far from uncommon. He begs Tacitus to send him well-qualified candidates from the number of those students who are attracted by admiration of his ability. But the choice he leaves free to the parents. We have no information how such schools were governed ; probably they were controlled by those who found the funds, whether these were the parents or the municipal council, with or without the help of endowments.

At a later date the Emperors took an even more direct part State Control in the control of the schools. Constantine by of Schools. edicts issued in A.D. 321, 326 and 333 conferred many privileges and exemptions on public teachers 'quo facilius liberalibus studiis multos instituant.' Julian in A.D. 362 asserts the right of the Emperor to revise the appointments to professorships. Hitherto it had been the exception for the Emperor to make the nomination himself; sometimes he had empowered some one else to nominate[1]; but usually the selection had been left to the local authority or curia. The remuneration of the teachers was probably, as a rule, fixed by the local authority, but even in the third century we find Constantius directing that at the revived school at Augustodunum (Autun) its head, Eumenius, should receive a salary of 600,000 sesterces. In A.D. 376, probably at the suggestion of Ausonius, who had been his tutor, the Emperor Gratian issued an edict which, while leaving the great towns free to appoint the teachers, fixed the salaries which were to be given. The teacher of rhetoric was to have twice as large a stipend as the teachers of grammar, whether Greek or Latin. But at Trèves, then the centre of the government of the province, somewhat higher salaries are prescribed. On the whole the position of a teacher at this time seems to have been one of considerable emolument and dignity, and a rhetorician of eminence like Ausonius might rise to high office in the State.

But though 'grammar,' *i.e.* literature, and rhetoric were
Results of pursued with much diligence on the traditional
School Training lines, there was little or nothing of the serious
in Grammar
and Rhetoric. and independent study of philosophy, still less of
science. The wide and comprehensive mental discipline, which Cicero and Quintilian had desiderated, was no longer even an ideal; and the narrower special training of the rhetorician had carried the day over the sounder training of the man of affairs. The servility which was learnt in the slavish imitation of the

---

[1] The edict by which Julian forbade any Christian to teach Greek literature had not of course any permanent effect; and was disapproved even by Pagans: cf. Amm. Marcell. xx. c. 10: 'illud autem erat inclemens obruendum perenni silentio, quod arcebat docere magistros, rhetoricos, et grammaticos, ritus Christiani cultores.'

classical models not unnaturally moulded the whole thought and combined with the political conditions of the time to stifle all true independence. In A.D. 425 an edict of Theodosius[1] and Valentinian made penal the opening of schools by persons unauthorised by the government.

We know a good deal about the schools of Gaul in the fourth century, mainly from the writings of the poet Ausonius, himself a teacher of grammar and rhetoric at Bordeaux; and we can see how strong and steady was the influence which they exerted on education. There was little literary productiveness, and what there was was marked by many serious faults. But at least great writers were studied and admired intelligently and a tradition of culture was maintained, until it was swept away by the irruptions of the barbarians.

'The defects of secular literature' in the fifth century after Christ 'can nearly all be traced to barrenness of thought and absence of sincerity and love of truth; and these again were the direct result of a school training the whole aim of which was to turn out imitators and masters of striking phrase[2].' Whether Ausonius would have had it in his power to effect any reforms in this system, as Mr Mullinger seems to think[3], may be left undetermined, and Sidonius was better fitted to illustrate the evil than to do anything towards removing it.

---

[1] When in 425 Theodosius II. founded what we may call the University of Constantinople, he provided endowments at the public cost for three Latin rhetoricians and ten Latin grammarians, five Greek rhetoricians and ten Greek grammarians, one philosopher and two jurisconsults. The proportions and the omissions equally surprise us; but law seems to have been considered sufficiently provided for by the great school at Berytus, and philosophy at Athens. Doubtless the range of miscellaneous knowledge which might be covered by a 'grammarian' was, as we have seen before, almost unlimited.

[2] Dill, *Roman Society in the Last Century of the Western Empire*, p. 369. The fundamental error had been hit long before by Seneca in his pregnant phrase, 'non vitae sed scholae discimus.'

[3] *Schools of Charles the Great*, p. 15.

The tradition of the Roman schools was overthrown only by the Frankish invasion and by the rise of the monastic schools of Cassian, whose *Institutiones*, early in the fifth century, were accepted as the rule for monastic life in Gaul. Under these a system of religious education was instituted, based upon distrust of, if not hostility towards pagan learning. The details do not concern us here. But neither the monastic schools nor the cathedral schools, which followed them on similar lines, took the place of the old municipal schools in maintaining the traditions of classical literature, and a genuine devotion to learning. When Charles the Great founded his Palace School, in which to train the sons of his nobles by liberal arts for the public service, he had to cross the sea to find a fit head for it, and place it under the charge of Alcuin of York. The old tradition was broken, though fragments of it long continued to be discernible, and have not ceased to do their share in shaping the aims and methods of education even to-day.

INDEX.

www.ingramcontent.com/pod-product-compliance
Ingram Content Group UK Ltd.
Pitfield, Milton Keynes, MK11 3LW, UK
UKHW042147280225
455719UK00001B/158

9 781107 600515